AI FUNDAMENTALS

Mastering the Basics of Artificial Intelligence

John A Robinson

Table of Contents

CHAPTER 1: INTRODUCTION TO AI

What Is Artificial Intelligence?

Artificial Intelligence (AI) has become increasingly prevalent in our daily interactions, manifesting in various forms such as face recognition on smartphones and tailored recommendations from online retailers. Simply put, AI encompasses the development of computer systems that can perform tasks traditionally associated with human intelligence, including speech recognition, facial recognition, problem-solving, and decision-making. This technology has woven itself into the fabric of daily life, influencing how we communicate, shop, and even seek medical care.

AI can be broadly classified into two categories: narrow AI and general AI. Narrow AI, as the name suggests, focuses on executing specific tasks with high levels of accuracy. Examples of narrow AI include voice-activated assistants such as Siri or Alexa, which are adept at understanding and responding to user commands but are not capable of operating outside their precise domains.

On the other hand, general AI aims for more ambitious aspirations, seeking to create machines with human-like intelligence that can adapt and reason across various tasks and domains. While we have not yet realized true general AI, research is actively progressing towards machines capable of learning and adapting in ways similar to human cognitive processes.

This chapter will explore the multifaceted world of artificial intelligence by examining its applications in everyday life, as well as the associated challenges and ethical considerations that arise as AI technology evolves.

Key Takeaways

- Artificial Intelligence is defined as computer systems capable of performing tasks that require human-like intelligence.
- The two main categories of AI are narrow AI, which specializes in specific functions, and general AI, which aims to emulate human-like cognitive abilities.
- AI applications are prevalent in various areas of daily life, such as virtual assistants and online recommendation systems.
- Ethical considerations surrounding AI include issues of privacy, bias, job displacement, and the need for accountability and retraining.

Narrow AI: Focused Intelligence for Specific Tasks

Narrow AI can be likened to a highly skilled expert who excels in a particular area, such as a fitness coach who specializes in health and fitness but lacks expertise in tax preparation. Narrow AI systems are crafted to perform designated tasks and solve specific problems exceptionally well. For instance, many users utilize narrow AI in the form of virtual assistants like Siri and Alexa, which can manage tasks, respond to questions, and even control smart home environments through voice commands.

Such narrow AI systems are developed using tailored algorithms and data specifically suited to their tasks, learning from vast information bodies to enhance their performance. However, a fundamental limitation of these systems is their inability to transfer knowledge or expertise across different domains. They are proficient within their trained parameters but cannot apply skills or learnings in other contexts.

Transitioning to General AI

As we investigate the next concept of general AI, we encounter a significant evolution in artificial intelligence. Unlike narrow AI's focus on specific tasks, general AI aspires to replicate human intelligence across diverse domains. This challenging pursuit involves creating machines that can engage in multiple tasks, understand complex concepts, and adapt swiftly to new situations. True general AI represents a comprehensive goal where machines could demonstrate the same reasoning, learning, and adaptability as human beings, advancing us towards a new era of intelligent machines free from limitations.

General AI: The Pursuit of Human-like Intelligence

Envision a landscape where machines possess intelligence equivalent to human cognitive abilities, capable of reasoning, learning, and solving problems. This vision encapsulates the ultimate aim of general AI—to develop systems that can operate across a vast array of tasks and domains, displaying human-like cognitive functions, including language processing, decision-making, and creativity.

Creating general AI is a daunting endeavor. It necessitates the formulation of algorithms that can interpret and respond to data from the surrounding world similar to human cognition. This includes adapting to experiences and environments without explicit programming.

The implications of achieving general AI are profound. Personal assistants could not only follow commands but could also anticipate user needs based on context and prior interactions. Autonomous vehicles may navigate roads instinctively like human drivers, enhancing road safety and efficiency. The potential applications are extensive and range from healthcare advancements to enhanced customer service.

Applications of AI in Daily Life

AI is rapidly infiltrating various aspects of our daily experiences. Simple tools, such as alarm clocks that analyze sleep patterns to wake you at optimal times, or the voice assistants mentioned earlier, display AI's transformative power in our routines. According to a survey conducted by Adobe, nearly half (48%) of consumers reportedly use an AI-powered device or service daily. From personalized streaming recommendations to virtual assistants, AI technologies are continuously improving efficiency and convenience in our lives.

AI's influence extends well beyond personal convenience; it is making notable strides in industries such as healthcare and transportation. In healthcare, AI algorithms analyze medical data to facilitate early disease detection, assist in surgical procedures, and develop customized treatment plans. In transportation, self-driving vehicles rely on advanced AI systems to interpret their environment and navigate safely, presenting the potential to minimize accidents and redefine transportation systems entirely.

Advancements in machine learning, natural language processing, and other AI technologies unlock new possibilities in integrating AI into various facets of our lives. As we witness accelerating growth in AI applications, we must also remain vigilant to the challenges and possibilities that accompany this progress.

Transition to Future Challenges and Opportunities

The future of AI presents a dual-edged sword—while the potential for remarkable advancements is pregnant with possibility, it is essential to navigate the ethical concerns that accompany such evolution. Focusing on improving algorithm accuracy and addressing bias in decision-making processes are crucial considerations as we integrate AI deeper into society. With focused, responsible development, we can harness the vast potential of AI while ensuring equitable access to its benefits.

The Future of AI: Challenges and Possibilities

As AI technologies develop, we are met with significant challenges alongside immense possibilities in terms of advancement. Ethical considerations are paramount as AI systems become increasingly capable. Addressing issues around privacy, bias, and accountability is essential, as harms can arise if not proactively managed.

Another challenge lies in AI's impact on employment. While AI offers opportunities for enhancing productivity through automation, it raises genuine concerns about job displacement. Many sectors already feel the impact of automation, making it necessary for businesses, governments, and educational institutions to focus on adapting and retraining workers threatened by AI technologies.

Despite these challenges, the horizon for AI is equally bright. Innovations in healthcare, transportation, and other sectors promise societal transformations. AI can enhance diagnosis and treatment strategies for healthcare professionals or optimize transportation systems to reduce accidents and congestion. The fulcrum for success is responsible development that harmonizes technological advancement with societal needs.

As we endeavor further into the ethical aspects of AI and how society can maximize the benefits, understanding these challenges is essential for shaping a future that is ethically grounded and constructive.

Ethical Considerations in the Development of AI

Navigating the emerging field of AI carries a significant responsibility concerning ethical implications. As we further develop AI technologies, establishing ethical guidelines becomes paramount for ensuring these systems are designed to benefit humanity.

Key Ethical Considerations

- **Privacy**: Given the increase in data collection through AI, protecting individual privacy is crucial. Establishing robust regulations around data usage is necessary to prevent unauthorized access and misuse.
- **Bias and Fairness**: AI systems learn from existing data sets; if this data contains biases or reflects societal prejudices, discriminatory outcomes can emerge. Developers must actively work to eliminate biases within algorithms and ensure equitable algorithms.
- **Transparency**: Many AI systems operate as "black boxes," creating mistrust among users. By aiming for transparency in how decisions are reached, developers can foster trust in AI systems.
- **Accountability**: In the event of AI causing harm or error, establishing clear accountability is vital. Developers should assume responsibility for adverse impacts of AI systems and work on corrective measures.

Addressing these ethical considerations early on can help shape a future where AI serves societal good while minimizing the risks involved.

Frequently Asked Questions

How does narrow AI differ from general AI in terms of capabilities and limitations? Narrow AI is capable of executing specific tasks effectively, while general AI aspires to perform any intellectual task that a human can undertake.

Can you provide examples of narrow AI applications currently used in various industries? Examples include voice assistants like Siri, self-driving vehicles, fraud detection in banking, recommendation systems in media, and customer service chatbots.

What are the main challenges faced in the pursuit of achieving general AI? Challenges encompass understanding human cognition, imitating emotional intelligence, and ensuring ethical deployment of AI technologies.

Are there potential risks associated with AI integration in daily life? Yes, potential risks include job displacement, privacy issues, biased algorithmic decision-making, and concerns about AI acquiring excess power or independence.

What ethical concerns arise during AI technology development? Ethical concerns, such as privacy rights, potential biases, and discrimination in systems like facial recognition, must be addressed throughout development.

Conclusion

Artificial intelligence stands as a fascinating and rapidly transforming paradigm in our world, influencing both routine activities and broader societal structures. From the narrow AI systems, such as voice assistants and recommendation engines, to our ongoing journey towards achieving general AI, the breadth and depth of its impact seem limitless.

As individuals navigate their daily lives, recognizing the pervasive applications of AI may deepen their appreciation for technology's capabilities. Be it through personalized content recommendations or emerging self-driving vehicles, AI consistently enhances user experiences.

While the promise of future advancements looms large, ethical considerations surrounding AI's widespread adoption require deliberate attention. As AI gains greater autonomy and integration into society, issues surrounding privacy, bias, and job displacement necessitate thoughtful deliberation. Balancing progress with responsible implementation is of utmost importance.

In summary, the journey of artificial intelligence merges historical milestones with future aspirations, from initial developments to current state-of-the-art technologies. As society further embraces AI's capabilities, maintaining vigilance on ethical impacts remains crucial. A bright future lies ahead, shaped by innovation interwoven with human values, driving progress that upholds dignity, equity, and respect as we navigate an AI-enhanced world.

Brief History of AI and Its Evolution

Artificial intelligence has a rich history spanning over half a century, undergoing transformations that have profoundly reshaped various industries and our daily lives. This section will provide an overview of AI's evolution, illustrating its journey through major milestones.

The Origins of AI: From Early Concepts to the Turing Test

The historical roots of AI can be traced back to the 1950s, a period marked by the budding development of computers. The term "artificial intelligence" was coined by John McCarthy in 1956 during a pivotal conference at Dartmouth College, which catalyzed AI research and exploration.

In the early days, researchers explored the conceptual framework of developing machines capable of reasoning, problem-solving, and even understanding natural language. A significant event entrenched in this exploration was Alan Turing's formulation of the Turing Test in 1950. This test sought to determine a machine's ability to exhibit intelligent behavior indistinguishable from that of a human, laying a critical foundation for future advancements in AI.

The AI Winter: Setbacks and Stagnation in the Field

AI experienced substantial challenges throughout its evolution, particularly during the period known as the "AI Winter." This era—characterized by stalled progress—was primarily driven by three factors:

1. **Lack of Funding**: As initial excitement surrounding AI waned, so did financial support for research. Investors withdrew their backing due to dwindling optimism regarding AI's potential, hindering ambitious projects.

2. **Unmet Expectations**: Early enthusiasm set high expectations for the capabilities of AI systems. When researchers faced fundamental challenges in replicating human-like performance, interest diminished, and disillusionment set in.

3. **Technological Limitations**: During this era, the available computational power fell short of the needs for advanced algorithms and neural network implementations. The lack of accessible technology prevented researchers from realizing significant breakthroughs or practical applications.

Despite the challenges faced during the AI Winter, this period ultimately indicated areas in dire need of improvement and reset pathways for future exploration.

Neural Networks and Machine Learning: A Turning Point for AI

The technological landscape shifted dramatically with the emergence of neural networks and machine learning, marking a pivotal turning point for AI. Neural networks, inspired by the structure of the human brain, consist of interconnected nodes that process information in a parallel fashion. They adaptively learn by modifying connections based on input data, enabling them to distinguish patterns and classify data effectively.

Neural networks, especially when combined with machine learning algorithms, have revolutionized diverse applications. They power advanced speech recognition systems, enabling tools like Siri and Alexa to better understand and process natural language. In computer vision tasks, such as image recognition and object detection, the deep learning techniques underpinning neural networks surpass traditional methods, resulting in unprecedented accuracy. Furthermore, these networks also hold promise in healthcare for applications like diagnostic support and drug discovery processes.

Deep Learning and Big Data: Fueling the AI Revolution

The explosive growth of both deep learning—a subset of machine learning—and big data has elevated the capabilities of AI to unprecedented levels. Deep learning relies on training intricate neural networks with extensive datasets, enabling systems to recognize patterns and draw insights that yield breakthroughs across various fields, including natural language processing and computer vision.

Big data is instrumental in advancing AI through the provision of rich datasets that necessitate analysis. Massive stores of structured and unstructured data facilitate deep learning processes, providing insights that enhance decision-making across industries. Organizations leveraging big data analytics can extract value from vast datasets swiftly, improving customer experience, optimizing operations, and exploring avenues for growth.

Current Applications and Future Possibilities of AI

Artificial intelligence is now intricately woven into the fabric of our daily lives. Self-driving cars utilize AI to navigate roadways, and virtual personal assistants help manage schedules through voice commands. AI-enhanced healthcare solutions assist physicians in making faster and more accurate diagnoses, while personalized education platforms cater to individual learning needs.

The potential applications of AI are vast and transformative. The future promises even more advancements spanning transportation, manufacturing, and entertainment. Continued research and development efforts will shape AI's trajectory, underlining the technology's role in enhancing productivity and innovating new solutions.

Frequently Asked Questions

- **What are the main challenges faced by AI researchers during the AI Winter period?** The AI Winter was marked by funding shortages, unmet expectations, and underwhelming computational capabilities that hampered progress.
- **How does deep learning differ from traditional machine learning algorithms?** Deep learning employs neural networks with multiple processing layers, allowing the automated extraction of features, while traditional machine learning often requires explicit programming.
- **What are current applications of AI in daily life?** AI actively influences daily life through various technologies, such as voice assistants, content recommendation systems, fraud detection, and healthcare diagnostics.
- **How does big data contribute to AI's advancement?** Big data fuels AI by providing extensive datasets needed to train and enhance algorithms, leading to more accurate predictions and informed decision-making.
- **What are potential ethical implications of AI in the future?** Future ethical concerns may arise from biased algorithmic decisions, privacy risks, and the overarching influence of AI on societal structures.

Conclusion

Over the course of this exploration, we have traversed a detailed history of AI evolution, from its nascent beginnings to its contemporary significance and future potential. Each chapter of AI's story holds valuable lessons and insights that could guide the development of responsible, ethical, and human-centered AI technologies.

From the successful applications of narrow AI, we encounter daily to the ambitious aspirations of general AI, artificial intelligence is on the brink of transforming numerous aspects of society. Acknowledging historical context, understanding current capabilities, and contemplating future trajectories can empower all stakeholders to navigate the challenges and seize the opportunities that arise, ultimately creating a future where AI serves humanity's collective well-being.

Basic Terminology and Concepts in AI

Navigating the intricacies of artificial intelligence can be daunting, but understanding fundamental terminology helps demystify the subject. By 2025, the global AI market is projected to reach an astounding $190 billion, highlighting AI's growing importance. Below are essential concepts that form the groundwork of AI technology.

Machine Learning: The Foundation of AI

Machine learning is the cornerstone of artificial intelligence, enabling systems to acquire knowledge and enhance performance through experience. It focuses on developing algorithms capable of learning from data inputs, making predictions or classifications without explicit programming.

By utilizing large datasets, machine learning algorithms can identify patterns, trends, and correlations that may be elusive to human observers. A tangible example includes spam filters that learn how to recognize unwanted emails based on labeled input provided by users.

Neural Networks: Mimicking the Human Brain

Neural networks emulate the sophisticated processes of the human brain. Composed of interconnected artificial neurons or nodes arranged in layers, neural networks process information through mathematical operations. They learn by adjusting connections based on input data, allowing them to optimize performance and minimize errors through training.

This principle of training a neural network employs a technique called supervised learning, where the network learns from labeled data to improve accuracy. By adjusting its internal parameters, a neural network can excel in various applications, including image analysis and natural language processing.

Natural Language Processing: Understanding and Communicating

Natural Language Processing (NLP) is a critical area of AI, enabling machines to comprehend human language. Through NLP algorithms, computers analyze and interpret spoken or written language. This capability allows machines to engage in activities ranging from automated customer service interactions to content generation.

Contextual understanding is essential in NLP, as machines must also recognize the meanings of words based on their surroundings. Thus, NLP trains systems on vast amounts of language data to enhance their interaction capabilities.

Computer Vision: Seeing the World through AI's Eyes

Computer vision is a discipline within AI that focuses on enabling machines to interpret and analyze visual data, including images and videos. Using advanced algorithms, computer vision enhances AI's ability to recognize objects, faces, and even emotional expressions.

Applications of computer vision are diverse, spanning industries such as healthcare, security, and transportation. For instance, self-driving cars employ computer vision to maneuver effectively in complex environments, while healthcare providers utilize it for diagnosing illnesses through imaging analysis.

Ethics and Bias in AI: Addressing the Impact of Artificial Intelligence

With the rapid infiltration of AI technologies into society, ethical considerations are paramount. AI raises questions regarding bias, privacy, and accountability in its applications. Here are some key areas to address:

- **Diverse Data Sets**: Ensuring that training data is representative of various demographics can help mitigate the risk of bias in AI systems.

- **Transparency**: Providers should be open about how AI systems operate, fostering accountability and enabling scrutiny.
- **Regular Auditing**: Conducting regular assessments of AI systems can help identify biases or unintended consequences, ensuring constant improvement.
- **Ethical Guidelines**: Establishing comprehensive ethical frameworks for developers to adhere to can prioritize fairness, privacy protection, and human rights.
- **User Feedback Loops**: Creating channels for user input can enhance AI's adaptability and responsiveness to diverse needs.

By comprehensively addressing ethical concerns, we can harness AI's profound capabilities while ensuring it serves society equitably.

Frequently Asked Questions

- **How does AI technology impact job opportunities and the workforce?** AI transforms employment landscapes by creating new roles while rendering some positions obsolete. Adjusting to these shifts is vital for workers in an AI-driven future.
- **Can AI technology be used to create realistic virtual environments or simulations?** AI is capable of constructing immersive virtual environments through realistic graphics and simulations, serving various purposes from gaming to training.
- **What are the potential risks associated with advancing AI?** Risks include job displacement, invasion of privacy, algorithmic bias, and concerns about the autonomy of AI systems increasing.
- **How does AI technology affect privacy and personal data protection?** AI's data-centric nature significantly impacts privacy; consumers express concern about mishandled personal data. Effective safeguards are essential for protection.
- **Can AI prevent or predict natural disasters?** AI can enhance disaster preparedness by analyzing data to predict potential threats, assisting in risk management and mitigation efforts.

Conclusion

This comprehensive examination of AI equips you with the foundational knowledge essential for engaging with this transformative technology. From machine learning's role as AI's backbone to natural language processing, neural networks, and computer vision, you have gleaned insight into AI's capabilities and its impact on society.

Furthermore, the ethical implications surrounding AI's development underscore the need for responsibility and vigilance. By recognizing AI as an augmentation of human capabilities rather than a replacement, we can embrace its potential while safeguarding core ethical values.

Armed with this understanding, you can confidently engage in discussions concerning AI, recognizing its promising trajectory as it continues to engage and redefine the boundaries of human experience. Embrace this ever-evolving field and let curiosity drive explorations into the realm of artificial intelligence, as opportunities for innovation and growth await. Together, humans and AI can forge a future celebrating creativity, ingenuity, and the betterment of society as a whole.

CHAPTER 2: HOW AI WORKS

Explanation of Machine Learning and Neural Networks

Machine learning is an essential process in the development of artificial intelligence (AI) systems, allowing machines to learn from data and improve their performance without explicit programming. This concept can be likened to instructing a child on how to ride a bicycle— initially, guidance and feedback are provided, but as they practice, they become skilled and learn independently.

In the realm of machine learning, algorithms analyze vast datasets to identify patterns and make predictions or decisions based on their acquired knowledge. This technology finds application in various fields including finance, healthcare, marketing, and beyond.

Key Takeaways

- **Machine Learning:** The process through which machines learn from data and improve their performance without being explicitly programmed.
- **Pattern Recognition:** Algorithms in machine learning analyze large volumes of data to discover patterns and make predictions or decisions.
- **AI Tasks:** Artificial intelligence utilizes machine learning algorithms to handle tasks that require human-like intelligence, such as understanding natural language and interpreting visual information.
- **Neural Networks:** These systems simulate the structure and functionality of the human brain and are potent tools for tasks like image recognition and natural language processing.

The Basics of Machine Learning

Machine learning functions by inputting a large volume of data into an algorithm, which examines the data to identify prevailing patterns. By recognizing these patterns, the algorithm creates a model, or a framework, that can be employed to make predictions or decisions regarding new data. This methodological process is referred to as training the model. The quantity and quality of data directly influence the model's ability to make accurate predictions.

Once a model has been adequately trained, it can be utilized to classify new instances or anticipate future outcomes, effectively acting on its learned knowledge.

Machine learning possesses a myriad of practical applications across diverse industries. In healthcare, for instance, algorithms can scrutinize patient records and medical imaging to identify diseases at their earliest stages or propose tailored treatment plans. In finance, machine learning models analyze historical trends and market data to forecast stock price movements or detect potential investment opportunities.

A strong grasp of machine learning fundamentals can enable individuals to utilize this technology efficaciously within their own fields.

Transition to Artificial Intelligence

With a fundamental understanding of machine learning established, let us transition to examining the broader concept of artificial intelligence, simplifying complex terminologies in the process.

Understanding Artificial Intelligence

Artificial intelligence refers to the creation of systems that can perform tasks typically requiring human cognitive functions, such as visual perception, speech recognition, and decision-making. As AI technology advances, we enter a realm where machines can think and reason similarly to humans, facilitating efficient problem-solving and decision-making capabilities.

Defining Key Aspects of AI

To better understand the landscape of AI, consider the following four core components:

- **Machine Learning:** Central to AI, machine learning facilitates computers' ability to learn from data and enhance performance over time, enabling them to adapt based on prior experiences.
- **Natural Language Processing (NLP):** AI systems utilize NLP techniques to comprehend and generate human language, which is vital for functionalities such as vocal assistants recognizing and responding to spoken commands.
- **Computer Vision:** Through computer vision, AI can interpret images and videos, enabling features such as facial recognition in security systems, object detection in autonomous vehicles, and medical diagnostics through imaging.
- **Robotics:** Integrating AI with robotics leads to the development of autonomous machines capable of performing tasks with minimal human intervention, from assembly line work to complex surgical procedures.

Applications of Machine Learning

Machine learning is deeply embedded in numerous facets of our daily lives, including personalized recommendations on streaming platforms and improved weather forecasting accuracy.

Healthcare Innovations

In healthcare, machine learning algorithms have proven instrumental. By analyzing extensive medical datasets, these technologies can uncover patterns that may not be readily noticeable to medical professionals. This capability aids in early disease detection and the customization of treatment strategies. The implications of integrating machine learning into healthcare are vast, potentially saving lives and enhancing patient care.

Financial Sector Enhancements

The financial services industry extensively leverages machine learning for fraud detection and algorithmic trading. Financial institutions harness machine learning algorithms to monitor transaction patterns, identifying anomalies that may signify fraudulent activity. This predictive capability has become essential, as it protects both financial entities and consumers from identity theft and fraud. Furthermore, algorithmic trading utilizes sophisticated models to analyze market movements, enabling informed investment decisions in real time.

Transformation in Transportation

The advent of self-driving vehicles has marked a significant transformation in transportation systems globally. These vehicles incorporate advanced machine learning algorithms that allow them to perceive their environment and navigate with precision. Drawing from extensive data sourced from sensors like cameras and radars, self-driving cars continuously enhance their operational capabilities. This technology holds the promise of minimizing human errors and subsequently elevating overall road safety.

Understanding Neural Networks

Neural networks serve as a fascinating component of machine learning, allowing for the processing and analysis of extensive datasets. Their architecture is designed to mimic the human brain's structure, comprising interconnected nodes, or neurons, that work collaboratively.

How Neural Networks Operate

Each neuron within a neural network receives input, processes it using mathematical functions, and outputs a signal, much like a human brain would handle sensory information. The synergy among neurons forms various layers in the network, enabling it to handle increasingly complex data.

Neural networks undergo a learning phase during which the strength of their interconnections is adjusted. As the network is exposed to labeled examples, it fine-tunes its internal parameters to accurately categorize new data. Therefore, the ability of neural networks to learn from data makes them incredibly effective tools for tasks ranging from image and speech recognition to natural language comprehension.

Evolution of Neural Networks

As research in neural networks progresses, advancements in architectures and algorithms continue to expand their capabilities. Ongoing innovations hold the potential to revolutionize numerous sectors, including healthcare diagnostics and autonomous driving.

Advancements in Artificial Intelligence

The pace of advancements in artificial intelligence mirrors the unearthing of a technological revolution, with AI's power to transform industries becoming ever more apparent. Modern AI has evolved significantly from its inception, continually expanding the boundaries of what is possible.

Key Areas of Progression

- **Deep Learning:** A notable advancement in AI is deep learning, which employs neural networks with multiple layers. This technique has yielded substantial breakthroughs in areas such as image recognition and natural language processing, allowing systems to learn directly from raw data.
- **Reinforcement Learning:** This innovative training paradigm encourages algorithms to learn from trial and error by rewarding successful outcomes and penalizing less favorable ones. This approach has led to incredible progress in robotics and complex movement tasks.
- **Generative Adversarial Networks (GANs):** GANs operate by positioning two neural networks in competition—one generates synthetic data while the other assesses authenticity. Through this dynamic, both networks enhance their performance, yielding remarkable capabilities in generating realistic images, music, and even video sequences.

As these advancements proliferate, the potential for AI to reshape our future becomes increasingly clear. Embracing these developments, while simultaneously addressing ethical considerations, is essential to unlocking AI's full benefits.

Frequently Asked Questions

How does machine learning differ from traditional programming?
Machine learning stands apart from conventional programming methods by enabling computers to improve through experience. It uses algorithms that detect patterns and make decisions based on accumulated data.

Can machine learning algorithms exhibit bias?
Yes, machine learning algorithms can reflect biases inherent in their training data, potentially leading to unfair outcomes.

What challenges arise in implementing machine learning applications?
Common challenges include the necessity for large amounts of high-quality data, issues surrounding bias and fairness, and concerns related to the interpretability of models.

How do neural networks manage incomplete data?
Neural networks address missing data through imputation techniques, estimating missing values based on available information.

What ethical considerations accompany machine learning use?
Ethical considerations in machine learning sphere encompass fairness, privacy, and accountability, ensuring technology serves its intended purpose without adverse societal effects.

Conclusion

In conclusion, a coherent understanding of machine learning and neural networks illuminates the foundations upon which modern artificial intelligence is built. It is vital to appreciate how these technologies impact our daily lives, from enhanced medical diagnostics to sophisticated recommendation systems.

The power of neural networks reveals an intricate and dynamic structure that mirrors the human brain's information processing. Ongoing advancements in AI technologies provide tantalizing glimpses into a future where machines learn and operate autonomously, changing the landscape of our interactions with technology.

Understanding the significance of training data—considered the fuel for machine learning—enables us to prioritize high-quality, diverse data collections. This requirement is paramount for creating robust machine learning models that respond effectively to new challenges.

Lastly, we converge on the ethical landscape surrounding AI. As we traverse this evolving field, it is imperative to uphold principles of fairness, transparency, and accountability, ensuring that the growth of AI technologies yields positive outcomes for society as a whole. Reflecting on these facets sets the stage for understanding the broader implications of machine learning and artificial intelligence in our interconnected lives.

Understanding Training Data and Algorithms

Training data serves as the indispensable precursor for machine learning models, functioning as the fuel that powers their learning capabilities. This data encompasses a broad array of examples or observations, which guide the algorithms in developing their decision-making processes.

The Role of Training Data

Training data plays a crucial role in teaching algorithms to recognize patterns and relationships inherent within it. By analogy, one can view training data in the context of academic instruction: just as students learn from diverse examples and discussions, algorithms benefit from rich datasets that provide varied perspectives.

Training data can take multiple forms, including text, images, or numerical values. For instance, if a model is tasked with identifying images of cats, it must be provided with a sufficiently large dataset of labeled images classified as "cat" or "not cat." The learning achieved through this process enables the algorithm to apply its acquired knowledge to unseen images.

In summary, training data is foundational to enabling machine learning algorithms to generate reliable predictions or classifications. Without high-quality input data, the learning process could falter, resulting in models lacking in accuracy.

Transition to Algorithms

Following our exploration of training data, we must delve further into the algorithms that drive machine learning, examining their intricate workings in detail.

The Role of Algorithms in Machine Learning

To comprehend the significance of algorithms in the realm of machine learning, one must recognize their integral function in processing data and generating insights. Algorithms serve as the computational engines behind the machine learning process, deriving new information from existing datasets.

Algorithms function by taking input data, manipulating it to discern patterns and relationships, and producing an output—often a prediction or classification based on the data analysis. This process involves employing various statistical techniques and mathematical models.

Given that distinct problems may require specific solutions, the choice of algorithm is pivotal. Algorithms designed for diverse tasks—such as image recognition or natural language processing—vary significantly in structure and function. Selecting the right algorithm ultimately determines the effectiveness of a machine learning model.

Thus, while the quality of training data is vital, so too is the careful selection of algorithms that align with the specific challenges at hand. Optimization of algorithms maximizes the performance of machine learning models in producing accurate predictions and meaningful decisions.

Transition to Quality Data

Having established the foundational role of algorithms in machine learning, we now turn our attention to the critical matter of data quality.

The Importance of Quality Training Data

Quality training data is paramount to achieving meaningful results in machine learning. High-quality data serves as the foundation upon which robust models are constructed, enabling algorithms to function effectively.

When considering training data, it is helpful to visualize a library filled with various books, with each book symbolizing crucial knowledge for training a model accurately. Just as literature can vary in quality, so too can the quality of training data affect outcomes. Ensuring that training data is free from biases and encompasses diverse examples is essential to obtaining reliable results.

A commitment to quality means providing algorithms with comprehensive datasets that represent a variety of scenarios. This diversity fosters robust learning and encourages models to behave more accurately in practice. Conversely, narrow or biased training datasets risk leading models to produce generalized and inaccurate assumptions.

Transition to Data Sources

With the importance of data quality recognized, we can now explore the various sources from which training data is drawn.

Types of Training Data Sources

The exploration of training data sources unveils a rich tapestry of avenues, each contributing to the development of machine learning algorithms. The following categories characterize the common types of training data sources:

- **Human-Generated Data:** This type of data arises from human input, often through manual labeling or surveying. Sources may include social media feedback, surveys, or direct observations, providing valuable insights into human behavior and preferences.
- **Machine-Generated Data:** As the name implies, machine-generated data is produced by devices or sensors, including telemetry data, logs, or sensor readings. This type of data is crucial in domains like robotics and autonomous vehicle training.
- **Simulated or Synthetic Data:** Artificially generated to replicate real-world scenarios, synthetic data permits researchers to test algorithms in controlled environments without introducing risk. Simulated datasets are particularly beneficial in areas like computer vision.
- **Publicly Available Datasets:** Numerous publicly available datasets suit various machine learning tasks, spanning topics like image recognition and natural language processing. They enhance accessibility to quality training data, democratizing opportunities for developers and researchers.

Recognizing these types of training data sources provides critical insight into how algorithms are nurtured through diverse experiences and simulated circumstances.

Transition to Real-World Applications

Understanding different training data sources accentuates the significant applications of these models in everyday life, impacting various sectors.

Applications of Training Data and Algorithms in Everyday Life

Training data and machine learning algorithms wield transformative potential across numerous industries, empowering continual innovation and improving daily experiences. For instance, platforms leveraging training data optimize user engagement through personalized recommendations, adapting to consumers' interests and preferences.

Healthcare Application

In healthcare, training data analysis contributes significantly to identifying patient patterns and predicting health issues. Machine learning models can process vast quantities of medical records swiftly, enhancing diagnostic accuracy and personalizing treatments. Additionally, research breakthroughs in drug discovery leverage extensive clinical trial datasets, accelerating innovations in therapies and medical interventions.

E-Commerce Enhancement

In the realm of e-commerce, algorithms tailor user experiences by analyzing purchasing behavior and demographic factors. E-commerce platforms effectively utilize historical data to suggest products aligned with users' preferences and behaviors. As a result, customers experience enhanced shopping interactions without unnecessary effort.

Societal Transformations

Training data and algorithms extend beyond individual sectors, influencing broad societal advancements. As technology evolves, its application in healthcare, finance, and transportation fosters increased efficiency, accuracy, and safety across diverse fields.

With a rich understanding of these applications established, we will now address some common inquiries related to machine learning and training data.

Frequently Asked Questions

How do algorithms process and interpret training data?
Algorithms interpret training data through statistical analysis, utilizing pattern recognition techniques to learn from data and make informed predictions or decisions.

What challenges can arise in working with training data?
Challenges with training data include data quality issues, the risk of bias, and the necessity for preprocessing to prepare data for effective analysis.

How do varying types of training data sources impact the accuracy of algorithms?
The accuracy of algorithms hinges on the diversity of training data. Real-world data generally provides a richer context for understanding, while synthetic data can facilitate controlled experimentation.

Can training data contain biases?
Yes, training data can embody existing biases. Such biases impact algorithm performance, often leading to skewed predictions or reinforcement of social inequities.

What ethical considerations arise in using training data and algorithms?
Ethical considerations in using training data and algorithms command attention toward privacy concerns, fairness, and transparency in data utilization.

Conclusion

To summarize, cultivating an understanding of training data and algorithms is crucial in navigating the contemporary landscape of machine learning. Awareness of the pivotal role training data plays in model effectiveness and the significance of algorithm selection enables practitioners to optimize outcomes.

Moreover, ensuring data quality remains paramount, as it serves as the basis for accurate predictions and reliable conclusions. Continuous attention to improving quality, accessibility, and ethical considerations will facilitate the responsible development and deployment of machine learning technologies, ultimately benefitting society at large.

The Role of Data in AI Systems

In the landscape of artificial intelligence, data functions as the vital medium fueling AI systems. This foundational asset informs the algorithms, guiding their learning processes and enabling them to make astute decisions.

How AI Systems Learn from Data

AI systems depend solely on data for learning, mirroring human experiences and observations. They require diverse and abundant datasets, which may consist of images, text, or sensory inputs relevant to the tasks they are designed to accomplish.

Through extensive data exposure, AI systems analyze each piece to discern patterns and derive actionable insights. This analytical process empowers them to recognize objects, translate languages, forecast financial trends, or even diagnose medical conditions. The efficacy of an AI system's performance is directly related to the diversity and comprehensiveness of the training datasets provided.

Transition to Data Diversity in AI

Recognizing that the caliber of data is not uniform leads us to understand the compelling need for diversity within AI training datasets.

The Importance of Diverse Data in AI

Diversity in data serves to enhance the effectiveness and accuracy of AI systems, allowing them to flourish within various contexts and adapt to a multitude of scenarios. The significance of incorporating varied datasets can be underscored by considering several key reasons:

- **Mitigating Bias:** By utilizing diverse data sources, AI systems can minimize biases that might surface from relying on uniformly sourced information. Multiple perspectives enrich learning opportunities, promoting fairer outcomes.
- **Enhancing Generalization:** Exposure to a wide array of examples enables AI systems to recognize overarching patterns across contexts. This strengthens their skill at generalizing knowledge beyond isolated incidents.
- **Bolstering Adaptability:** In an evolving technological landscape, varied data inputs equip AI systems to navigate new scenarios effectively. By embracing different data types, these systems can be more responsive to unanticipated changes.
- **Fostering Creativity:** Engaging with diverse data encourages innovation within AI. By encountering varied datasets, these systems forge unique connections among concepts, yielding creative solutions and insights.

Transition to Data Processing in AI

Understanding the necessity of diversity in data leads us to explore the methodologies by which AI processes large datasets.

Data Processing in AI Systems

To appreciate how AI systems manage and analyze vast datasets, we must consider the stages of data processing they employ. This sequence often includes:

- **Data Collection:** Initially, AI systems gather relevant data from an array of sources, encompassing text, images, audio, and sensory data.
- **Data Preprocessing:** Collected data undergoes cleaning and organization to prepare it for further analysis. This step is pivotal to ensure the data is suitable for the model training phase.
- **Feature Extraction:** In this phase, AI systems identify critical patterns and characteristics within the data. For instance, in image recognition tasks, edge detection or texture analysis helps differentiate objects.
- **Model Training:** The extracted features are utilized as inputs during the model training process. Models learn complex relationships between input data and output predictions by analyzing vast datasets.

Ultimately, the efficiency of these algorithms hinges on the diversity and quality of the training data. A well-trained model can accurately interpret new inputs based on prior experiences.

Transition to Enhancing AI Performance

Enhancing the capabilities of AI systems through meticulous data analysis plays a monumental role in optimizing both accuracy and efficiency.

Enhancing AI Performance through Data Analysis

Data analysis encompasses the examination of collected information to discern patterns, correlations, and trends that might be overlooked. This scrutiny allows us to glean deeper insights and refine the functionality of AI systems.

Through detailed data analysis, we can identify areas where AI systems underperform or err. By revisiting training datasets, we can uncover biases or limitations that hinder performance. Such exploration facilitates the optimization of AI systems by recalibrating parameters or integrating new features to address identified weaknesses.

Additionally, employing advanced techniques such as anomaly detection affords us the capacity to pinpoint data irregularities that signal potential issues within an AI system.

Transition to Ethical Considerations

Given the transformative potential of data analysis, it is essential to also recognize the ethical implications accompanying data-driven AI systems, particularly concerning user trust and privacy.

Ethical Considerations in Data-driven AI Systems

Exploring the ethical considerations associated with data-driven AI systems brings to light critical issues that impact trust and privacy.

- **Data Collection and Use:** Data-driven AI systems frequently operate using extensive data, prompting questions about how this information is sourced and whether user consent has been given. Ensuring that robust safeguards are in place to protect sensitive personal information is vital.

- **Potential for Bias:** Given that AI systems learn from historical and existing datasets, there exists a risk of perpetuating biases present within the data. For example, recruitment algorithms that draw from historically biased hiring practices may reinforce systemic discrimination, leading to inequitable outcomes. Regular audits of AI systems are essential to identifying and mitigating such biases.

- **Transparency and Accountability:** Clarity regarding how user data is collected, stored, and utilized by AI systems fosters an environment of trust. Mechanisms should exist enabling users to access and modify their information. Furthermore, organizations responsible for deploying AI technologies must accept accountability for unintended negative consequences arising from their use.

In summary, ethical considerations surrounding data-driven AI systems demand vigilance and proactive management. Addressing the need for personal data protections and working vigilantly against bias are essential steps toward maintaining trust in technology.

Understanding these ethical considerations allows us to address common queries that arise concerning the usage of data-driven AI systems.

Frequently Asked Questions

Which types of data can AI systems learn from?
AI systems are capable of learning from diverse data sources, including images, text, audio, and more, enriching their understanding and aiding decision-making.

How does data diversity enhance AI effectiveness?
Diverse datasets improve the robustness of AI systems, allowing them to learn comprehensively and develop decision-making capabilities that account for varying contexts.

What involves the data processing steps in AI systems?
Data processing in AI systems typically entails gathering relevant data, preprocessing it to ensure suitability, extracting significant features, and training algorithms to make predictions.

How can data analysis enhance AI performance?
Through data analysis, we can identify trends and outliers, refining algorithms and enhancing overall predictive accuracy.

What ethical considerations must be addressed when deploying data-driven AI systems?
When utilizing data-driven AI systems, ethical considerations involve addressing privacy, ensuring fairness and transparency, and promoting accountability in data handling.

Conclusion

In conclusion, data serves as the linchpin for AI systems, empowering them to learn, adapt, and evolve. A thorough understanding of the importance of diverse and comprehensive training data informs better model performance and paves the way for responsible AI development.

Recognizing the intensive processing of data through systematic approaches contributes to enhanced capabilities in AI systems. Nevertheless, ethical implications surrounding data use must be a primary focus to ensure responsible practices that benefit society.

Through intentional efforts to prioritize quality, diversity, and ethical standards in data utilization and AI development, we can harness the vast potential of these technologies while cultivating trust and equity in their application across society.

CHAPTER 3: PRACTICAL APPLICATIONS OF AI

AI in Everyday Life: Virtual Assistants, Recommendation Systems, and More

Artificial Intelligence (AI) has become an integral component of our daily routines, profoundly influencing the way we interact with technology. Virtual assistants such as Siri and Alexa serve as prime examples of how AI enhances our everyday experiences. These intelligent systems utilize Natural Language Processing (NLP) to comprehend and respond to the commands issued by users, significantly improving how we communicate with machines. As we go about our daily tasks, it is essential to understand the technology driving these virtual companions and the breadth of their capabilities.

Virtual assistants operate through sophisticated NLP algorithms that analyze both spoken and written language. By employing these algorithms, virtual assistants can distinguish between different commands, understand user intent, and execute tasks with increasing efficiency. Whether a user seeks directions, sets a reminder, or engages in casual conversation, these AI-driven assistants are becoming increasingly adept at meeting our needs in intuitive ways.

The Development of Virtual Assistants

The journey of virtual assistants began with Apple's introduction of Siri in 2011, marking the arrival of a new era in personal technology. Siri was one of the first major virtual assistants, and it could perform simple tasks such as sending messages, making calls, or setting reminders. However, its capabilities were limited in terms of understanding complex commands and engaging in natural dialogue.

Fast forward to the present day, and we now have advanced virtual assistants such as Amazon's Alexa, Google Assistant, and others, which can seamlessly integrate into our lives. These enhancements result from ongoing research in fields such as machine learning and deep neural networks. These technologies empower virtual assistants not only to understand and process information but also to learn from past interactions, improving their functionality over time.

As a result, these virtual companions now assist users with a wide range of tasks, from providing weather forecasts and controlling smart home devices to playing music and offering personalized recommendations. The evolution of virtual assistants signifies a shift towards a more connected and efficient lifestyle, wherein technology is not just a tool but an indispensable ally.

Key Takeaways

- **Virtual assistants** like Siri and Alexa utilize NLP to understand and respond to user commands, enhancing user interactions.
- **Continuous learning** enables these assistants to adapt to individual preferences and improve task efficiency.
- **Recommendation systems** leverage past behavior to generate personalized suggestions in areas such as online shopping and entertainment.
- Both virtual assistants and recommendation systems contribute significantly to improving everyday experiences through tailored services.

The Functionality of Virtual Assistants

The extensive functionality of virtual assistants contributes to their role as essential tools in our daily lives. These AI-driven companions excel in aiding users with a multitude of tasks, helping to streamline day-to-day activities. Their capabilities extend from basic functions, such as setting reminders and answering questions, to more complex tasks like controlling smart home devices or delivering personalized content.

At the heart of their functionality lies NLP technology, which allows virtual assistants to comprehend spoken language and respond accordingly. This capability enables them to interpret user requests accurately and provide relevant information in real-time. For instance, when a user inquiries about the weather for the next day, the assistant utilizes NLP algorithms to decode the request and retrieve the corresponding forecast.

Moreover, virtual assistants leverage machine learning algorithms, which empower them to evolve based on user interactions. By analyzing past conversations, these systems can tailor their responses according to individual preferences, enhancing the user experience. For instance, they may recommend nearby restaurants based on previous dining habits or curate personalized playlists based on listening history.

As such, virtual assistants play a crucial role in simplifying our daily routines by bringing cutting-edge technological solutions within reach through user-friendly interfaces. This seamless interaction exemplifies how these AI entities are redefining our engagement with technology, making tasks simpler and more efficient than ever before.

Natural Language Processing: How Virtual Assistants Understand Us

Natural Language Processing (NLP) serves as the backbone for virtual assistants' understanding of human language. This branch of AI focuses on the interaction between computers and human communication, enabling machines to interpret text and speech in a meaningful manner.

NLP comprises various processes, including phonetic analysis, syntactic parsing, semantic understanding, and discourse analysis. Through these methodologies, virtual assistants can dissect sentences into smaller components, analyze their structure, and comprehend the contextual meaning behind user queries. This allows them to match user inputs with pre-existing knowledge or external resources to deliver accurate and relevant information or execute tasks.

The evolution of NLP has propelled virtual assistants from basic question-and-answer systems to sophisticated conversational interfaces capable of holding natural dialogues with users. These advancements continue to evolve alongside innovations in machine learning and data processing capabilities, ultimately enriching the user experience.

The Evolution of Virtual Assistants: From Siri to Alexa

The progress of virtual assistants over the years represents a significant leap in AI technology, particularly in understanding and responding to human interactions. Siri's launch marked the beginning of a transformation, but the emergence of more advanced systems like Amazon's Alexa has illustrated the potential of conversational AI.

Alexa distinguished itself through its ability to interpret intricate commands and engage in more interactive dialogues. Beyond basic tasks like playing music or providing weather updates, Alexa can control an array of smart home devices in real-time, showcasing its adaptability across different contexts. Its extensive training involving diverse datasets has enabled it to accurately comprehend various accents and dialects, further solidifying its user-friendliness.

This evolution in AI technology has paved the way for a new standard in user interaction. Today's virtual assistants have evolved into indispensable companions, capable of understanding individual needs and preferences while providing personalized recommendations. Such capabilities enhance user satisfaction and foster a sense of connection between technology and its users.

The Power of Recommendation Systems

Recommendation systems have become a cornerstone of modern technology, driving user engagement and wellbeing in various industries. These intelligent algorithms analyze vast amounts of data to deliver personalized suggestions of products, services, or content that align with individual preferences.

Functionality of Recommendation Systems

The functionality of recommendation systems can be outlined through the following steps:

- **Understanding Preferences**: Recommendation systems collect historical data about user behavior, such as purchases, likes, and interaction history. Analyzing this data enables the system to create a precise profile of user interests.
- **Identifying Patterns**: Once the system has a comprehensive understanding of user preferences, it looks for patterns among similar users. By comparing behaviors and interests, the system can identify potential items or content that a user may appreciate.
- **Making Personalized Suggestions**: Armed with the knowledge of user preferences and patterns, the recommendation system generates tailored suggestions. These recommendations reflect popularity, user trends, and availability, ensuring relevance.
- **Continuous Learning**: Recommendation systems are designed to learn from users' feedback continuously. This adaptability ensures the system evolves alongside changing preferences, enabling it to provide increasingly relevant suggestions.

Through these capabilities, recommendation systems play a crucial role in enhancing user experiences across various platforms. They streamline decision-making, simplify content discovery, and ultimately foster deeper engagement with products, services, and experiences.

Personalized Suggestions: How Recommendation Systems Enhance Our Experiences

Recommendation systems have dramatically transformed our interactions with digital platforms, converting them into uniquely personalized experiences. By tapping into user data, these systems can analyze previous behaviors, such as the articles read, movies watched, and music streamed. Such understanding enables tailored recommendations that resonate with individual interests.

This personalization is particularly evident in online shopping environments like Amazon, where users may encounter sections titled "Recommended for You" or "Customers Who Bought This Also Bought." These suggestions are curated by algorithms that assess user behavior in tandem with broader trends, yielding personalized recommendations that enhance the shopping journey.

Similarly, music streaming services such as Spotify utilize sophisticated algorithms to create tailored playlists based on user listening patterns. By analyzing previous likes and plays, these platforms provide users with fresh content that aligns with their musical tastes, enriching the overall listening experience.

Thus, recommendation systems increase our ability to discover new products, content, and experiences that align with our unique preferences. By leveraging AI to analyze vast datasets, these systems enhance our digital interactions and lead to a more fulfilling engagement with various platforms.

AI in Healthcare, Finance, Transportation, and Other Industries

Artificial intelligence's reach extends beyond virtual assistants and recommendation systems; it is transforming numerous industries, including healthcare, finance, and transportation. In these sectors, AI technologies enhance operational efficiency, improve decision-making processes, and ultimately facilitate better service delivery.

Applications of AI in Healthcare

AI is making significant strides in healthcare, producing remarkable advances in patient care. By leveraging machine learning algorithms and data analysis techniques, AI can assist healthcare providers in multiple ways:

- **Medical Diagnostics**: AI systems can analyze extensive medical data, including patient records and diagnostic results, yielding timely and accurate insights. This capability enables healthcare professionals to make better-informed decisions and personalize treatment plans based on individual patient needs.
- **Medical Imaging**: AI algorithms are increasingly utilized to analyze various medical images—such as X-rays, MRI scans, and CT scans—with superior precision. These systems can identify abnormalities or signs of disease that human radiologists may overlook, facilitating early diagnoses and enhancing patient outcomes.
- **Virtual Healthcare Assistants**: AI-driven chatbots and virtual assistants can help streamline patient interactions by gathering symptoms, providing medical advice, scheduling appointments, and even offering emotional support. Their round-the-clock availability alleviates some burden on healthcare professionals, allowing them to prioritize critical responsibilities.

As we explore the transformative potential of AI in sectors such as finance and transportation, it becomes evident that this technology is set to redefine our lives and industries.

AI's Impact on the Finance Industry

Within the finance industry, AI is playing a critical role in streamlining transactions, enhancing risk management, and preventing fraudulent activities. The following highlights some key areas in which AI is making an impact:

- **Transaction Efficiency**: AI algorithms can analyze vast datasets quickly, executing transactions with unprecedented accuracy. This capability reduces the likelihood of errors and delays associated with manual processes.
- **Risk Management**: AI has revolutionized risk assessment by continuously monitoring market trends. Through data analysis, it can identify potential risks and anomalies, enabling financial institutions to proactively address issues before they escalate.
- **Fraud Detection**: AI-powered systems are adept at spotting suspicious patterns and behaviors, dramatically reducing fraudulent activities. By continuously assessing transaction data, these algorithms can enhance security and prevent financial losses.
- **Optimizing Investment Strategies**: AI technologies empower investors by providing invaluable insights into historical performance and market trends. Machine learning algorithms continually adapt and evolve, making it easier for investors to allocate resources and manage their portfolios effectively.

Through these advancements, AI is driving transformative changes in the finance industry, enhancing overall efficiency, risk management, and informed decision-making.

AI in Transportation: Revolutionizing the Way We Travel

In transportation, AI is reshaping how we travel by creating a future where daily commutes become more efficient and enjoyable. The implementation of AI technologies has led to significant innovations:

- **Self-Driving Cars**: Autonomous vehicles equipped with advanced sensors and algorithms can navigate roads and anticipate real-time traffic patterns. These systems can reduce human error, enhance road safety, and streamline traffic flow.
- **Intelligent Routing Systems**: AI also enables intelligent routing solutions that analyze real-time data to optimize travel routes. By considering factors such as traffic congestion and public transportation schedules, commuters can save time and enhance their travel experiences.
- **Virtual Assistants in Vehicles**: AI-powered virtual assistants integrated into vehicles can deliver personalized recommendations for dining, entertainment options, and efficient routes tailored to individual preferences. This personalization further enhances traveler satisfaction and experience.

As AI technology continues to evolve, our journeys will become increasingly seamless and tailored to individual needs. Each advancement reinforces the potential of AI to revolutionize not only our personal lives but also vital industries.

Exploring AI in Various Industries

The applications of AI span a multitude of sectors, from retail to customer service to manufacturing. In each of these areas, AI is utilized for automating tasks, analyzing data for insights, and enhancing efficiency.

- **Retail**: AI algorithms optimize inventory management, personalize marketing efforts, and enhance customer engagement through tailored recommendations and promotions.
- **Customer Service**: AI-driven chatbots and virtual assistants are becoming commonplace, providing real-time support to customers while allowing human agents to devote their attention to more complex inquiries.
- **Manufacturing**: In manufacturing, AI assists in predictive maintenance, enabling companies to reduce downtime by anticipating equipment failures. This enhances overall productivity and efficiency within production processes.

As these examples illustrate, AI is redefining how various industries operate and interact with their customers, driving innovation and improving service delivery.

Benefits and Potential Risks of AI Implementation

While the benefits of AI implementation are substantial, it is crucial to also recognize the potential risks associated with its integration into various industries:

Benefits of AI Implementation

- **Increased Productivity**: AI automates mundane tasks, allowing human workers to focus on higher-value activities that require creativity and strategic thinking.
- **Error Reduction**: AI systems perform repetitive tasks with a high degree of accuracy, minimizing human errors typically associated with fatigue or distraction.
- **Enhanced Decision-Making**: AI analysis of vast datasets results in more informed and timely decisions, empowering organizations to respond quickly to shifting conditions.
- **Personalized Customer Experiences**: AI enables companies to tailor services and recommendations based on exhaustive user data, greatly enhancing customer satisfaction.

Potential Risks of AI Implementation

- **Job Displacement**: Automation could lead to job loss in certain sectors as AI systems take over tasks traditionally performed by humans. Employees may need to reskill to remain relevant in the evolving job market.
- **Privacy Concerns**: The handling of sensitive personal information through AI systems raises ethical concerns about data security and privacy, necessitating robust measures to safeguard user information.
- **Bias in Decision-Making**: AI technologies can inadvertently incorporate biases based on their training data, leading to skewed decision-making processes. This highlights the need for transparency and thorough testing to mitigate bias.
- **Dependence on Technology**: As organizations increasingly rely on AI-driven systems, there is a risk of diminished human oversight, resulting in over-reliance on technology that may not account for nuanced situations.

Conclusion

The integration of AI into our lives, from virtual assistants to recommendation systems, has fundamentally altered the way we interact with technology and the world around us. By empowering users with personalized experiences and enhancing the efficiency of various industries, AI technologies have revolutionized everyday tasks.

As illustrated throughout this chapter, AI offers immense potential across various sectors—including healthcare, finance, and transportation—by improving efficiency, decision-making, and overall service delivery. However, it is paramount to navigate the potential risks associated with AI with a thoughtful approach. This includes promoting ethical applications of AI, considering the implications of job displacement, and safeguarding privacy and security.

As AI continues to advance and mature, it is paramount that organizations strike a balance between harnessing the benefits of these technologies while prioritizing ethical considerations and the human experience. Ultimately, the responsible implementation of AI will lead to a future where technology not only enhances our lives but also upholds our values and principles.

CHAPTER 4: THE POWER OF DATA

Importance of Data in AI Development and Decision-Making

In the contemporary landscape of technology, data functions as the cornerstone of artificial intelligence (AI) development and decision-making. It is essential for the understanding of AI algorithms and for enhancing their operational capabilities, demonstrating its significance at every phase of AI evolution.

When considering AI development, think of data as the fundamental building blocks. It forms the bedrock on which AI algorithms are constructed and trained. These algorithms are designed to process and learn from extensive datasets, extracting patterns, making predictions, and performing a wide array of tasks. Without ample and diverse datasets, AI lacks the ability to comprehend intricate concepts or accurately analyze information. Thus, possessing comprehensive and varied datasets is paramount for effective AI training.

However, the importance of data goes beyond mere quantity. The quality of data plays a pivotal role in augmenting the capabilities of AI systems. When developers input precise and reliable data into AI systems, it significantly enhances the system's ability to learn from accurate sources, consequently leading to informed decision-making. This, in turn, improves the effectiveness, accuracy, and overall performance of AI technologies across numerous sectors, such as healthcare, finance, and transportation.

This section will delve into the pivotal role that data plays in AI development and decision-making in straightforward terms. We will examine how data fuels the creation of AI algorithms, exploring why comprehensive datasets are integral to training these systems effectively. Additionally, we will discuss the ways in which quality data enhances artificial intelligence technologies and influences their decision-making capabilities. Let us explore the profound influence of data in the realm of artificial intelligence.

Key Takeaways

- High-quality data is critical for AI to make informed choices and deliver valuable insights.
- Access to accurate information enables AI to analyze emerging patterns, trends, and understand complex scenarios.
- A diverse and well-structured dataset helps AI technologies mitigate biases, facilitating fair and ethical decisions.
- Extensive data allows AI algorithms to learn from past experiences, adapt to new conditions, and make precise predictions.

The Role of Data in AI Development

The role of data in AI development cannot be overstated. Data is akin to fuel for AI systems. Just as a vehicle requires fuel to operate, AI algorithms need data to learn and make decisions. Absent data, AI would exist as a hollow entity devoid of knowledge or understanding.

By analyzing vast volumes of data, AI systems can uncover patterns, identify trends, and ultimately generate accurate predictions. Data serves as a foundational element in training AI models. To illustrate, consider it like feeding a starved machine with essential information; the more varied and eclectic the data, the more proficient the AI model becomes in recognizing diverse patterns and making informed choices.

To further clarify, teaching someone how to drive without practical examples or real-space experience would yield poor comprehension of navigating road conditions. Likewise, an AI model starved of sufficient and relevant data would struggle to grasp complex tasks or scenarios.

Understanding the intricacies of AI algorithms in conjunction with data processing is vital for leveraging the power of data in AI development. This involves engineers designing AI algorithms capable of efficiently processing massive data volumes while accurately extracting meaningful insights. Such processes include detecting patterns within datasets, categorizing information, and forecasting future outcomes based on historical trends. By utilizing well-structured algorithms alongside high-quality datasets, we can unlock the paramount potential of artificial intelligence in delivering intelligent decisions.

In summary, data is not merely important; it is integral to the development of AI. Without it, no sophisticated artificial intelligence systems could be constructed.

Understanding AI Algorithms and Data Processing

To navigate the domain of artificial intelligence successfully, one must grasp how AI algorithms function and how they process information. Understanding AI algorithms resembles having a recipe for effective decision-making. Just as recipes delineate the necessary ingredients and their proportions, AI algorithms dictate the data that should be analyzed and how to interpret that data.

This systematic process enables machines to make predictions or decisions informed by patterns within the data.

For example, suppose you aim to train an AI system in identifying cats within images. Initially, you would feed the algorithm a series of labeled images featuring both cats and non-cats, allowing it to comprehend the distinguishing features of each. Following this, during the training phase, the algorithm would distill these images into smaller components known as pixels and assess various statistical measurements for each group of pixels.

Subsequently, using these measurements, the algorithm would ascertain whether a given image contained a cat. When presented with unfamiliar images, the algorithm would apply previously acquired knowledge from the training data to identify the presence of a cat.

Thus, it becomes evident that a comprehensive understanding of AI algorithms is insufficient; access to broad and diverse datasets is equally crucial. The true power of AI emerges from having a substantial array of examples that encapsulate different contexts and scenarios.

Datasets that incorporate various cat breeds depicted from differing angles and under various lighting conditions enhance accuracy in identifying cats in real-life situations. By utilizing detailed and diverse datasets, AI systems can render more informed decisions founded on prior experiences with analogous examples.

The Power of Comprehensive and Diverse Datasets

The true potential of artificial intelligence is revealed through a rich and varied dataset that equips machines to develop a nuanced understanding of complex patterns and to make informed judgments.

In training AI algorithms, the availability of comprehensive and diverse datasets is fundamental. Consider a scenario where an AI system is only endowed with a narrow range of data, offering a limited perspective or biased viewpoint. This would severely hinder its capacity to accurately interpret and analyze real-world situations.

By providing AI systems with comprehensive and varied datasets, we bolster their ability to learn from an extensive compilation of examples and scenarios. For instance, in training an AI algorithm for image recognition, employing a dataset that features images captured from multiple sources, angles, lighting conditions, and demographic variables ensures that the AI system can accurately identify objects across various contexts.

Moreover, diverse and comprehensive datasets also play a significant role in minimizing biases in the decision-making processes undertaken by AI systems. By exposing these systems to a mix of perspectives and experiences through data, we can diminish the risk of biased, discriminatory outcomes.

For instance, in the context of AI employed for hiring, utilizing a diverse dataset that represents candidates across a broad spectrum can assist in reducing potential biases based on gender or ethnicity by ensuring that the system has been trained on data encompassing a wide array of candidates.

By leveraging comprehensive and diverse datasets to train AI algorithms, we enable machines to attain a better understanding of complex patterns, empowering them to generate informed judgments. These datasets create an opportunity for learning from various examples and perspectives prevalent within society while simultaneously helping to reduce bias.

Enhancing AI's Capabilities through Quality Data

Employing high-quality datasets allows artificial intelligence to unlock its full potential, facilitating the perception of intricate patterns with artist-like precision and executing insightful judgments akin to seasoned detectives.

Similar to an artist who requires a range of colors on their palette to create a masterpiece, AI algorithms necessitate diverse and comprehensive data sources to learn effectively. Feeding AI systems with well-curated datasets that encompass varied scenarios and perspectives equips them to succeed in multifaceted tasks—be it image recognition, speech comprehension, or predicting future trends.

Quality data acts as the driving force behind AI, enabling machines to learn from past encounters and adjust their decision-making methodologies accordingly. Analogous to detectives amassing evidence from various sources to solve intricate cases, AI relies on the presence of high-quality data to make informed choices.

Through access to a vast reservoir of accurate and reliable information, AI can analyze patterns and trends across extensive datasets with remarkable efficiency. This capability allows it to discern underlying connections between variables that might elude human observers.

The significance of utilizing quality data profoundly impacts AI decision-making. Armed with reliable information, artificial intelligence evolves into a more trustworthy entity, adept at providing meaningful insights. High-quality data ensures that the decisions made by AI systems are grounded in accurate knowledge rather than prejudice or incomplete understanding.

In addition, by integrating diverse perspectives into the training datasets, we reduce the likelihood of bias in decision-making procedures and augment the fairness of results.

The Impact of Data on AI Decision-Making

Harnessing the strength of properly curated datasets reveals the vast influence that data possesses over the decision-making abilities of artificial intelligence. When AI systems are furnished with substantial and diverse high-quality datasets, their accuracy and reliability in decision-making improve significantly.

The abundance of data empowers AI algorithms to uncover patterns, assess correlations, and predict outcomes with a precision that often exceeds human capabilities. Data fundamentally shapes AI decision-making processes, providing the vital information that algorithms require to analyze and comprehend intricate situations.

In practical terms, this can be seen in the context of autonomous vehicles. Data collected from sensors—such as cameras and radars—enables AI systems to recognize objects, detect obstacles, and make split-second decisions essential for safe navigation. Without a thorough set of datasets, AI would face challenges in accurately interpreting its environment and making informed decisions.

Moreover, the quality and diversity of data constitute significant factors affecting fairness and ethical considerations in AI decision-making processes. Incomplete or biased datasets can lead to discriminatory outcomes or actions executed by AI systems. Therefore, it is imperative for developers to ensure that their models are trained on a wide array of datasets that reflect real-world contexts, steering clear of reinforcing existing biases.

Data serves as the lifeblood of AI decision-making. Properly curated datasets allow AI to learn from historical experiences, adapt to novel scenarios, and perform tasks with impressive accuracy. Nonetheless, developers and organizations leveraging AI technologies must remain vigilant about the quality and diversity of their data sources to guarantee equitable outcomes while avoiding discrimination.

Harnessing the potential of data-driven decision-making presents remarkable opportunities for innovation, necessitating responsible management of this invaluable resource.

Frequently Asked Questions

How does the quality of data impact the development of AI algorithms?

The quality of data has a substantial impact on the development of AI algorithms, significantly influencing the accuracy and reliability of their outputs. High-quality data allows AI systems to make informed decisions and generate trustworthy results.

What are the key factors to consider when selecting and preparing a dataset for AI development?

When preparing datasets for AI development, factors such as data accuracy, relevance, diversity, and size should be prioritized. These aspects ensure that AI algorithms function effectively and can make informed decisions.

Can AI algorithms be effective without comprehensive and diverse datasets?

No, AI algorithms cannot function effectively without comprehensive and varied datasets. Such datasets provide the necessary information foundational for the algorithm to learn and make accurate decisions. Without them, the performance of the algorithm is severely restricted.

How does the accuracy and reliability of data influence AI decision-making?

The accuracy and reliability of data profoundly impact AI decision-making. Inaccurate or unreliable data can result in flawed or incorrect decisions, leading to unreliable outcomes.

Are there any ethical considerations related to the use of data in AI development and decision-making?

Ethical considerations in AI data usage arise from potential biases and discrimination present in the data. For example, statistics reveal that facial recognition systems misidentify people of color disproportionately, exposing risks involved in making decisions based on flawed data.

Conclusion

In conclusion, understanding the crucial role that data plays in AI development and decision-making is vital. Without quality data, AI algorithms function akin to a ship adrift without direction. The undeniable power of comprehensive and diverse datasets establishes a foundation for effectively training AI models to make accurate predictions and informed decisions.

Harnessing the data's potential enhances AI capabilities and unlocks its full potential. Much like a finely tuned machine, AI thrives on high-quality data that fuels its learning processes. Each piece of data it encounters enhances its ability to analyze and comprehend the world.

As you embark on the journey of developing AI systems or relying on their decision-making ability, keep in mind this essential principle: "Do not place all your eggs in one basket." By ensuring that AI has access to diverse and comprehensive datasets, we empower it to make rounded, well-informed decisions.

AI Data Collection Methods and Concerns about Privacy

AI systems acquire information from various sources, including user interactions and sensor-based data collection techniques. These methodologies yield valuable insights that contribute to the improvement of AI algorithms and the enhancement of user experiences.

User interactions provide multifaceted data sources for AI systems. When you engage with websites, applications, or devices, every action—clicks, search queries, or messages—is meticulously recorded and analyzed. For instance, when utilizing a search engine or making an online purchase, AI algorithms gather data about your preferences and behaviors. This ability enables companies to tailor their services, providing personalized recommendations uniquely suited to you.

In addition, sensor-based data collection represents an emerging method for AI systems to gather information. Devices such as smartphones and smartwatches track user behavior and the surrounding environment. These sensors monitor various metrics—location, physical activities, and more—to provide comprehensive insights into user habits. While these techniques may raise concerns about privacy, they also play a vital role in enhancing AI capabilities.

However, even as AI technology progresses, legitimate privacy concerns accompany data collection. Protecting personal information becomes increasingly critical in this era of rapid technological advancement. Companies must handle collected data with responsibility, implementing robust security measures and adhering to privacy regulations.

As consumers, it is essential to remain mindful of the information being collected, how it is utilized, and who has access to it. Striking a balance between technological advancement and the safeguarding of personal privacy becomes paramount as we navigate the expanding landscape of AI-driven innovations.

Key Takeaways

- AI systems collect user interaction data from websites, applications, and devices, in addition to sensor-driven data.
- Privacy concerns arise from the potential misuse of personal information by AI algorithms and through sensor-based data collection.
- Organizations must handle collected data with care and enforce robust safeguards to protect individuals' personal information.
- Individuals should be cognizant of the information being gathered, how it is employed, and their ability to manage their data among AI systems.

User Interactions as Data Sources

As users navigate websites and communicate with chatbots, their actions and conversations contribute valuable data sources. Each interaction—a click, search query, or message—accumulates into a vast pool of information that companies analyze to better understand user preferences and behaviors.

As an example, when engaging with a virtual assistant or browsing an online retail platform, remember that your interactions generate copious amounts of data that drive the algorithms behind these services.

Nonetheless, what does this mean for user privacy? Although data collection can enhance service provision, it also provokes valid concerns regarding the handling of personal information. Conversations may contain sensitive information that individuals might not wish to divulge. Additionally, the amalgamation of various data points can create detailed profiles that raise questions about surveillance and potential misuse of power.

Consequently, it is vital for organizations to maintain transparency concerning their data collection methodologies. Using strong security measures to protect user privacy becomes essential in the development of AI technologies.

Transitioning to the subsequent section about **sensor-based data collection**, it is important to note that user interactions represent just one facet of the overall data collection picture. Sensor-based techniques rely on the gathering of information from physical devices, including smartphones and wearables. These devices can monitor location, movements, and biometric indicators—without necessitating direct user involvement.

By analyzing sensor data in conjunction with user interactions, AI systems can extract deeper insights regarding individuals' behaviors and tendencies.

Sensor-Based Data Collection

Sensor-based data collection refers to the utilization of various devices that capture environmental information, thereby enabling us to glean valuable insights and recognize intricate patterns. Everyday objects—like smartphones, smart speakers, and security systems—are embedded with sensors that continuously gather data passively.

Examples of sensor-based data collection methods include:

- **Camera Surveillance:** Cameras situated in public places, or even in residential areas, capture images or videos that can be analyzed to discern traffic patterns or detect intrusions.
- **Microphone Monitoring:** Smart speakers, such as Amazon Echo and Google Home,

listen for voice commands but might also capture ambient noises to enhance their speech recognition algorithms.

- **Location Tracking:** GPS-enabled devices consistently collect location data, aiding navigation. However, this raises concerns about privacy violations.
- **Health Monitoring:** Wearable devices, including fitness trackers and medical apparatuses, gather data related to heart rate, sleep patterns, and other health indicators. While these measures assist in monitoring personal health, they also provoke concerns regarding access to sensitive facts.
- **Environmental Sensing:** Sensors positioned throughout cities can measure air quality, noise pollution, and other environmental factors. While this information helps municipalities identify areas in need of improvement, it also compels scrutiny regarding privacy.

As technology advances and becomes deeply integrated into lifestyles, sensor-based data collection will increase. However, the implications of constant monitoring on individual privacy require thoughtful consideration. Ensuring the protection of personal information must take precedence while developing such technologies, providing individuals with control over their data and their knowledge of its use.

Safeguarding Personal Information

In this digital era, protecting personal information has become increasingly vital, particularly in light of the constant data gathering performed by technology. As aspects of our lives shift online, safeguarding personal details from misuse or unauthorized access becomes more critical every day.

Safeguarding encompasses not only basic information, such as names, addresses, and contact numbers, but extends to sensitive data, including health records and financial details.

There are several steps users can take to protect their personal information:

- **Mindfulness of Online Activity:** Individuals should pay attention to the websites and apps they engage with, ensuring they have secure connections (indicated by a padlock symbol in the URL bar) and reviewing their privacy policies to understand how data will be collected and utilized.
- **Strong Password Practices:** Creating robust, unique passwords for each account is crucial. Easily guessable passwords, such as "123456" or "password," should be avoided.
- **Regular Updates:** Keeping devices regularly updated with new software and applications will help to maintain current security patches.

Although implementing these precautions can mitigate the risks associated with personal information exposure, it remains essential to recognize ongoing privacy concerns linked to AI data collection. The vast amounts of information harnessed by AI raise fundamental questions about access and usage rights.

Discussions regarding these issues will be further explored in the next section on privacy concerns in AI data collection methods.

Privacy Concerns in AI Data Collection

To gain deeper insights into AI's influence on our lives, it is worth contemplating a reality wherein every scroll, click, and online acquisition is recorded and processed by intelligent systems. These systems gather enormous quantities of data, encompassing browsing history and social media actions, aimed at unveiling our preferences and tendencies.

While such capabilities may appear beneficial—resulting in personalized recommendations and tailored user experiences—they also elicit serious privacy concerns. It is alarming that our personal data could be misappropriated or utilized for purposes without our consent. There exists a considerable risk of potential misuse and abuse of collected information.

Furthermore, there are apprehensions that AI algorithms may exacerbate biases and discrimination due to their reliance on historical data that can reflect societal prejudices. Given the swift development of technology, maintaining a balance between advancements and protecting personal privacy is essential.

Policymakers and organizations must establish clear guidelines and regulations surrounding AI data collection practices. Striking a harmony between harnessing AI capabilities and upholding individual privacy rights is paramount in fostering trust within these systems.

Balancing AI Advancements with Privacy Protection

Achieving the right balance between advancing AI technology and protecting personal privacy undeniably presents challenges. On one hand, the potential benefits of AI innovations—ranging from healthcare to transportation—are profound. On the other hand, the reliance on data collection raises significant privacy issues. It is vital to find a balance facilitating technological advancement while also ensuring protection of individuals' private information.

Several considerations should be taken into account to achieve this equilibrium:

- **Transparency:** Companies and organizations should maintain transparency about their data collection practices and how this information is utilized. Clear explanations of AI systems and obtaining explicit consent from individuals is essential before collecting personal data.
- **Anonymization:** Efforts ought to be made to anonymize collected data wherever possible. By removing personally identifiable information (PII), linking specific data back to individuals becomes increasingly difficult.
- **Data Minimization:** Organizations should prioritize the collection of only essential data, thereby mitigating privacy risks by minimizing the amounts of personal information required for AI training or analysis.
- **Security Measures:** Robust security practices must be implemented to shield stored data from unauthorized access. This includes encrypting data, utilizing secure storage methods, and conducting regular security audits.
- **User Control:** Individuals ought to have control over their own data, possessing the ability to access and delete personal information from AI systems as desired.

Considering these elements and instituting privacy-centric practices alongside AI enhancements allow us to ensure that technological advancements proceed in tandem with protecting personal privacy in this digital era.

Frequently Asked Questions

How is user interaction used as a data source in AI data collection?

User interaction serves as a valuable data source for AI, providing insights into user preferences, habits, and behaviors. Statistical evidence suggests that around 70% of users' online activities can drive improvements in AI algorithms to deliver personalized recommendations.

What are some examples of sensor-based data collection methods used in AI?
Sensor-based data collection methods encompass various techniques such as GPS tracking for location data, accelerometer and gyroscope usage for motion detection, environmental monitoring through temperature and humidity sensors, and image recognition via cameras.

How can personal information be safeguarded in AI data collection?
Safeguarding personal information in AI data collection necessitates employing encryption to limit access to authorized individuals, thus minimizing the risk of privacy breaches.

What are some privacy concerns associated with AI data collection?
Concerns associated with AI data collection encompass the risk of personal data being misused or shared without consent, potential discrimination due to biased algorithms, and the lack of transparency in data collection practices.

How can we balance the advancements in AI with the protection of privacy?
Striking a balance between AI advancements and privacy safeguarding involves implementing well-defined regulations and guidelines. This ensures the protection of personal information while supporting continued innovation and progress in AI technology.

Conclusion

This exploration of AI data collection methodologies alongside their associated privacy concerns has illuminated understanding in layman's terms. As users, each interaction with various platforms and devices serves as a crucial data source, shaping AI capabilities. Every click, every voice command, every piece of information contributes to an ever-expanding reservoir of knowledge.

However, this reality also brings concerns regarding privacy. It is imperative that organizations handle user data responsibly and implement rigorous safeguards to prevent unauthorized access or misuse. Understanding privacy concerns, users should be aware of the nature of collected information and how it is used within AI systems.

While advancing AI technologies offers exciting prospects, achieving equilibrium between innovation and privacy protection represents a delicate balancing act. As much as we value personal privacy, we equally appreciate the personalized experiences AI offers. Therefore, finding creative means to anonymize and aggregate data while simultaneously delivering tailored services without compromising individual privacy remains a pivotal challenge.

Navigating the intricate landscape surrounding AI data collection mandates a proactive approach to safeguard personal information, ensuring the benefits of technological advancement are maximized while protecting individual rights. It is crucial to remain cognizant that every interaction contributes to an ever-growing repository of knowledge—one that users must feel comfortable engaging with.

Data Bias and Ethical Considerations in AI Systems

In the complex domain of AI systems, data plays an integral function. Nevertheless, it is essential to recognize that the data employed to train these systems may encompass inherent biases. Such biases can emerge from various factors, including historical inequalities or human prejudices manifested during the data collection process.

Consequently, when AI systems base their decisions on biased data, they risk perpetuating existing inequalities or discriminating against specific demographic groups—often unintentionally. Gaining a comprehensive understanding of the implications of data bias on AI decision-making is critical for ensuring fairness and preventing harm caused by biased AI outcomes.

Ethical considerations form another vital dimension of AI system development. Although technology evolves at an accelerated pace, it is imperative to align these advancements with core values and ethical principles. Ethical matters within AI development concern issues such as invasion of privacy, algorithmic accountability, and transparency.

Addressing these ethical dilemmas is essential for averting the misuse of AI technology and safeguarding individual rights. Moreover, our development efforts should prioritize fairness and inclusivity, ensuring that all individuals benefit equally from these technological advancements. By employing relatable language to discuss ethical implications, we can enhance the understanding of users concerning how their data is utilized while promoting responsible practices within the AI sector.

Key Takeaways

- Data bias can arise in AI systems from historical inequalities and human prejudices present within the data collection process.
- Biased data can lead to discriminatory decision-making and further entrench existing inequalities.
- It is essential to promote fairness and inclusivity within AI development to ensure equal advantages for all stakeholders.
- Transparency and accountability are paramount in addressing ethical issues associated with AI development.

Understanding Data Bias in AI Systems

A robust understanding of the complexities surrounding data bias within AI systems is crucial. When contemplating artificial intelligence, many people associate it with objective and impartial decision-making mechanisms. However, the effectiveness of AI systems is inherently tied to the data that informs their training. If this data is biased or deficient, AI systems will inevitably reflect those biases in their outcomes.

Data bias can be conceptualized as unfairness or favoritism embedded within the training data of an AI system. Various factors can give rise to bias, such as historical discrimination, human prejudices, or inaccuracies in the data collection process. For instance, if an AI system relies predominantly on male voices in training voice recognition technology, it may struggle to accurately identify the nuances in female voices due to a lack of diverse training data.

Recognizing and addressing data bias is crucial, as it directly affects the outcomes initiated by AI systems. If an AI system learns from biased data, it will inadvertently replicate discriminatory patterns in its decision-making processes. Therefore, recognizing and mitigating these biases is essential for ethical and fair AI technology application.

As this understanding deepens, it becomes increasingly necessary to examine how data biases influence the results generated by AI systems. By doing so, we can formulate strategies aimed at cultivating more equitable and inclusive AI systems that benefit all, rather than perpetuating existing societal biases.

The Impact of Data Bias on AI Decision-Making

The presence of skewed information within the input utilized to train AI models can significantly impact the decisions made by these systems. When AI is trained on biased data, it tends to amplify such biases in its decision-making processes.

As an illustration, consider a facial recognition system primarily trained on images of white individuals. This specific training may hinder its ability to accurately recognize and classify the faces of individuals with darker skin tones, potentially leading to discriminatory outcomes and unfair treatment of particular demographic groups.

Further highlighting the impact of data bias, consider a recruitment algorithm trained using historical employment data. If such data reflects existing biases regarding hiring practices—like favoring male candidates over equally qualified female candidates—the algorithm will unwittingly learn and replicate such biases. Consequently, when evaluating job applicants, the system may prioritize male candidates over female applicants solely based on their gender.

The implications of biased AI decision-making are far-reaching and hold significant real-world consequences for individuals and communities alike. Such bias can entrench societal disparities, exacerbate discrimination, and reinforce existing inequalities across various sectors, including criminal justice, healthcare, finance, and education.

Given the increased reliance on AI systems that make critical decisions impacting people's lives, it becomes imperative to proactively address these issues, ensuring fairness and equity throughout our society.

Moving forward, addressing ethical concerns in AI development requires not only acknowledging the presence of data bias but also implementing tangible measures to mitigate its adverse effects. Strategies such as collecting diverse datasets, conducting rigorous bias detection tests during model development, and establishing transparent evaluation processes can help cultivate ethical AI systems that yield fair outcomes without amplifying pre-existing societal prejudices.

Addressing Ethical Concerns in AI Development

Effectively addressing ethical concerns surrounding AI development involves proactively considering the potential ramifications posed by biased data, while undertaking measures to ensure fairness and equity in decision-making processes. It is essential to recognize that AI systems reflect the biases inherent within their training data. Therefore, developers must thoroughly analyze and comprehend these biases to prevent their effects from propagating throughout AI decision-making.

This endeavor includes implementing strict testing and validation processes aimed at exposing any discriminatory patterns or biased outcomes. Furthermore, developers should include diverse perspectives when designing and training AI systems. Collaborating with a varied team helps to identify and resolve potential biases during the development process.

Additionally, enlisting the input of ethicists, social scientists, and other professionals provides critical insights into ethical challenges that may emerge throughout development. By actively seeking diverse viewpoints, developers can better inform their decision-making regarding the broader implications of AI systems on individuals and communities.

Ultimately, tackling ethical concerns in AI development demands a commitment to transparency and accountability. Developers should disclose the limitations of their AI systems, including any biases or uncertainties associated with those systems. Furthermore, establishing concrete guidelines for the responsible use of AI technology can aid in mitigating unintended consequences and discouraging unethical behavior.

Through promoting fairness and inclusivity in AI systems, we can contribute to the development of technological advancements that positively impact all stakeholders, ensuring equitable benefits derived from these innovations.

Promoting Fairness and Inclusivity in AI Systems

Promoting fairness and inclusivity in AI technology necessitates integrating diverse perspectives and expert insights throughout its design and development phases. Establishing fairness requires a diverse team of developers who represent various backgrounds and experiences. Including individuals from differing ethnicities, genders, cultures, and socioeconomic statuses can facilitate the identification of biases more effectively and address them during the development process.

Inclusivity in AI systems can further be enhanced by incorporating stakeholders from marginalized communities into decision-making processes. Engaging these individuals allows for valuable input regarding how AI technologies may affect their communities. By actively considering their insights and needs, it becomes possible to avoid inadvertently harming or excluding certain groups of individuals.

By fostering engagement with these stakeholders throughout the development cycle, we contribute to creating systems that honor equity and respect diversity. Incorporating these diverse perspectives aids in developing AI systems that are fairer and more inclusive for all users.

However, achieving fairness within AI systems is an ongoing endeavor, reflecting the evolving nature of societal norms. Continuous assessment of AI systems is necessary to detect potential biases or unintended consequences that could affect various demographic groups. To ensure that ethical considerations remain central to AI development, vigilance and adaptability must be prioritized.

Transition: Ensuring Ethical Considerations in Layman's Terms

To ensure that ethical considerations are integrated into AI development without delving into overly complicated language or technical jargon, we can adopt an informative approach.

One effective means of promoting ethical considerations within AI systems is through transparency. Developers should be open and forthright about the operational mechanics of their AI systems, encompassing data utilization, algorithms employed, and any existing biases. Transparency facilitates a clearer understanding for users regarding decision-making processes, who can then hold developers accountable for potential disparities or unfairness.

Another significant facet of ethical consideration in AI systems is the inclusion of diverse perspectives during the development process. Soliciting contributions from experts across various domains—such as ethics, social sciences, and humanities—yields insights into biases and ethical dilemmas. Moreover, seeking input from marginalized communities allows developers to circumvent further entrenchment of existing inequalities.

Conducting regular audits and assessments of AI systems is likewise critical in identifying any ethical concerns or biases that could arise over time. While these evaluations should encompass technical details, they must also provide a comprehensive overview regarding the societal implications of these systems. By continuously monitoring and assessing AI systems against ethical standards, developers can rectify any issues that surface and ensure ongoing alignment with ethical guidelines.

Ensuring ethical considerations in AI systems involves prioritizing transparency regarding data usage and decision-making processes. Moreover, it requires fostering diverse perspectives throughout the development process and conducting regular audits to assess bias and unethical outcomes. By adhering to these practices and conveying ethical principles in accessible language, we can work toward mitigating bias and fostering fairness in AI technology for the benefit of all stakeholders.

Frequently Asked Questions

How can data bias impact the decision-making process of AI systems?

Data bias significantly shapes AI decision-making processes, as biased training data can yield unfair or discriminatory outcomes based on inherent prejudices embedded in the data.

What are some ethical concerns that arise in the development of AI systems?

Ethical concerns in AI development include privacy infringement, discrimination, and displacement of jobs. Addressing these concerns must be a priority to ensure that AI technology is harnessed for societal benefit without causing harm.

How can AI developers address and mitigate data bias in their systems?

Developers can confront data bias in AI systems through thorough analysis and investigation to better evaluate potential biases, proactively implementing measures to ensure fairness and inclusivity.

What steps can be taken to promote fairness and inclusivity in AI systems?

To promote fairness and inclusivity, actions can be taken such as guaranteeing diverse representation during the developmental process, routinely auditing for biases, enhancing transparency and accountability, and actively engaging input from affected communities.

What are some practical ways to ensure ethical considerations are met when developing AI systems?

To ensure ethical considerations in AI development, one must thoughtfully engage with diverse perspectives, carry out rigorous testing, and establish clear guidelines that dictate responsible AI use.

Conclusion

In summarizing the importance of recognizing data bias within AI systems, we highlight the profound implications it holds for decision-making processes. As metaphorical fishermen casting nets into the sea, AI algorithms depend upon extensive datasets to formulate predictions and choices, but if these nets are tainted with biases, then the resultant decisions will similarly be flawed.

Consider this analogy: standing at a crowded intersection, awaiting the traffic light's transformation, you spot an AI-assisted vehicle. This vehicle deploys sensors and algorithms to evaluate the situation, identifying a quartet of pedestrians crossing the street. However, if the data informing its training predominantly reflects one racial or gender demographic, the algorithm may inadvertently prioritize specific individuals over others, reflecting biases from its training data.

To address these ethical challenges, the focus must shift toward promoting fairness and inclusivity within AI systems. This entails actively collecting diverse training data covering wider demographics, ensuring that AI algorithms genuinely represent society as a whole.

Furthermore, transparency regarding algorithms and decision-making processes is of paramount importance, enabling users to comprehend underlying logic and providing avenues for feedback and corrections when warranted.

It is critical for not only experts but also everyday individuals to grasp these ethical considerations and communicate them in plain language. Such understanding empowers society to challenge biased AI systems encountered across various aspects of life, whether during hiring processes or in the criminal justice system.

By collectively addressing data bias and advocating for fairness within AI technology, we can aspire towards an inclusive future, enabling artificial intelligence to benefit all members of society without perpetuating inequality or discrimination.

CHAPTER 5: UNDERSTANDING MACHINE LEARNING

Supervised, Unsupervised, and Reinforcement Learning

The field of artificial intelligence (AI) has captivated the curiosity of many. One of the core methods by which machines learn from data and make autonomous decisions employs three primary algorithms: supervised learning, unsupervised learning, and reinforcement learning. Each of these approaches offers distinct methodologies and applications for problem-solving that are essential to grasping the vast potential of AI technologies.

Supervised Learning

Supervised learning serves as a foundational method in the realm of machine learning. It is analogous to a traditional educational system where a teacher guides students through lessons, providing them with labeled examples. In this paradigm, the dataset consists of inputs paired with explicit outputs. The primary objective of the model is to uncover the relationship between these inputs and outputs so it can make informed predictions or classifications for new, unseen data.

For example, an apparent application of supervised learning is in email spam detection. Here, a model is trained on a dataset containing numerous emails, some identified as 'spam' and others as 'not spam.' The model learns to extract relevant features from the emails, such as specific keywords or sender information, and uses this information to classify new emails. When the model encounters a new email, it utilizes its learned patterns to determine its relevance as spam or legitimate mail.

By consistently comparing its predictions against the actual labels, the model refines its parameters to boost its predictive accuracy. The iterative learning process is fundamental for enhancing the model's performance and reliability in real-world applications.

Unsupervised Learning

Contrasting sharply with supervised learning, unsupervised learning does not use labeled data. Instead, it explores datasets where the algorithm has no predefined outcomes to guide its learning. This method is similar to an explorer navigating an unknown territory, identifying patterns and structures without any imposed direction.

Unsupervised learning offers several methods:

- Clustering: This entails grouping similar data points based on their characteristics. For example, clustering techniques can be used in market segmentation to identify distinct customer groups within a dataset based on purchasing behavior and demographics.
- Dimensionality Reduction: This technique simplifies complex datasets by reducing the number of variables while preserving essential information. An example is Principal Component Analysis (PCA), which helps visualize high-dimensional data by projecting

it onto lower-dimensional spaces.

- Association Rules: This approach uncovers relationships between different items within a dataset. For example, market basket analysis in retail may identify that customers who purchase bread also tend to buy butter. Understanding such associations can significantly influence marketing strategies and inventory management.

By leveraging unsupervised learning techniques, researchers and practitioners can derive meaningful insights and uncover latent patterns in large datasets.

Reinforcement Learning

Distinct from both supervised and unsupervised learning, reinforcement learning hinges upon the concept of trial and error. It is predicated on the interaction of an agent with its environment and the feedback it receives based on its actions. In this scenario, the learning agent receives rewards for achieving specified goals or suffers penalties for undesirable actions, thus refining its behavior over time to maximize cumulative rewards.

Consider the analogy of playing a video game where you navigate through a maze to collect points while avoiding obstacles. Initially, the player may not know optimal strategies or paths. However, through repeated trials, they learn which actions yield the best outcomes. This iterative process enables the reinforcement learning algorithm to develop strategies that improve its performance within the environment.

Reinforcement learning has garnered significant attention for its applications in various fields. In robotics, for instance, agents can learn to navigate complex terrains by simulating scenarios until they refine their movement strategies. Similarly, in the realm of self-driving vehicles, these algorithms are pivotal in enabling cars to make real-time decisions based on sensor input and environmental feedback.

The growing prominence of reinforcement learning reflects its vast potential for practical applications, extending beyond gaming into critical domains such as healthcare, logistics, and business operations.

Real-World Applications of AI

The transformative power of AI manifests in numerous applications across a variety of industries. Everyday tasks that once required significant human effort are increasingly being automated and enhanced through intelligent systems. Consider the following notable examples:

- Virtual Assistants: AI-powered assistants like Siri and Alexa utilize natural language processing to comprehend user commands, enabling them to perform diverse tasks such as setting reminders, playing music, or providing information. These systems rely heavily on machine learning algorithms to understand and respond to user queries effectively.
- Healthcare: AI has made profound inroads in healthcare, where it enhances diagnostics and treatment options. Machine learning algorithms analyze extensive datasets encompassing medical records, research papers, and imaging results to identify patterns generally overlooked by human practitioners. For instance, AI can assist in detecting diseases in imaging studies, ultimately enabling earlier intervention.
- Autonomous Vehicles: The integration of AI in transportation is exemplified by self-driving cars. These vehicles employ machine learning algorithms paired with sensors and cameras to gather real-time data about their surroundings. This information

guides their navigation, allowing them to make informed decisions about acceleration, braking, and lane changes, thus improving road safety and traffic efficiency.

These examples underscore the growing ubiquity of AI-powered solutions and their potential for enriching daily life.

The Future of Machine Learning

The landscape of machine learning is continuously evolving, fostering innovation across diverse fields. As technology progresses, one can expect several advancements that will redefine the functioning of machine learning and its applications.

- **Advanced Healthcare**: The integration of machine learning in healthcare can revolutionize patient care. Emerging applications include predictive analytics for early disease detection, personalized treatment plans, and advanced robotic surgeries. The ability to analyze vast volumes of data will lead to more effective treatments and improved patient outcomes.

- **Smart Cities**: The implementation of machine learning into urban infrastructure is paving the way for the development of smart cities. Analyzing data from sensors that track traffic flow, energy consumption, and public safety can optimize resource allocation. This capability holds tremendous promise for enhancing the living standards of urban dwellers.

- **Autonomous Vehicles**: The future of transportation lies in fully autonomous systems, where machine learning will continue to play a critical role. The development of delivery drones and automated public transport will likely become more prevalent, efficiently navigating complex environments while prioritizing safety.

- **Personalized Experiences**: The power of machine learning in creating personalized experiences will become increasingly pronounced. From entertainment recommendations to targeted advertising, these systems will cater to individual preferences, enhancing user engagement across various domains such as education and virtual reality.

While the potential for machine learning is exhilarating, it is crucial to navigate these advancements with ethical considerations in mind. Issues related to privacy, algorithmic bias, and the impact on employment due to automation remain paramount concerns. As society moves forward, finding a balance between innovation and responsible AI development will be essential.

How AI Learns from Data and Improves Over Time

AI systems exhibit remarkable capabilities to train themselves through data analysis, including pattern recognition and prediction formulation. This continuous learning process facilitates ongoing improvements in accuracy and efficiency.

Training AI with Data

The initial phase of AI learning involves feeding large datasets into the system. Much like humans gain knowledge from experience, AI models learn by evaluating numerous examples and relating them to specific tasks. The quality and quantity of the data are paramount to the learning process. Effective learning occurs only when the data are diverse and relevant, allowing the model to generalize its findings effectively to new scenarios.

For example, to train an AI model for image recognition, it is essential to curate a dataset that encompasses a wide variety of images, including variations in angles, lighting, and contexts. By doing so, the model can develop a robust understanding of the object characteristics it is meant to identify.

The iterative feedback loop in AI training is a critical mechanism. When the model makes predictions based on the training data, it compares these outcomes against known labels to determine accuracy and adjust its parameters accordingly. This refinement process is fundamental for enhancing the model's predictions over time, optimizing its performance.

Recognizing Patterns and Making Predictions

The ability of AI systems to recognize patterns is akin to a detective piecing together evidence to unravel a mystery. An AI model sifts through extensive datasets, identifying recurring trends and correlations that can be indicative of future outcomes. This predictive power can lead to substantial advancements in various sectors.

For instance, in e-commerce, AI can analyze consumer behavior trends to forecast what products may likely appeal to specific demographics. These predictions empower businesses to tailor their marketing strategies effectively, enhancing customer satisfaction and driving sales.

The capacity for AI systems to recognize subtle patterns often surpasses human capabilities. By analyzing vast datasets at incredible speeds, these systems can uncover insights that would otherwise remain concealed to human analysts. This functionality serves as a testament to the growing sophistication of AI technologies.

Continuous Improvement through Data Analysis

AI systems are not static entities; they evolve through continuous analysis of incoming data. Key aspects of this improvement cycle include:

- **Data Collection**: AI systems aggregate data from diverse sources, encompassing multiple formats such as text, images, and audio. This variety enriches the learning experience, aiding the model in developing a multifaceted understanding of the task at hand.
- **Pattern Recognition**: After data collection, AI models engage in rigorous analysis to extract patterns, correlations, and relationships. This ability enables them to make predictions informed by past observations.
- **Feedback Loop**: Post-prediction, models undergo a comparison process, measuring their predictions against actual outcomes. Discrepancies prompt adjustments to enhance future performance, ensuring a continuous learning trajectory.
- **Adaptation through Machine Learning**: Advanced adaptation techniques, such as deep learning, enable AI systems to iterate on their models based on new data inputs. Continuous learning allows the systems to develop new insights and enhance their capabilities over time.

The intricate relationship between continuous data analysis and AI performance improvement reflects the dynamic nature of these systems. Their relentless pursuit of learning from new information opens doors to innovative applications that can tackle complex challenges.

Understanding Neural Networks

At the heart of many AI systems lies the concept of neural networks, powerful algorithms structured to mimic human cognitive processes. Neural networks consist of interconnected layers of nodes, or "neurons," where each neuron performs computations and passes information to the subsequent layer.

This architecture enables the network to learn from data while adapting its internal parameters. The process of training neural networks involves the iterative adjustment of weights and biases linked to each neuron through various techniques. One predominant approach, known as backpropagation, establishes a feedback loop that informs the network of errors, allowing it to learn and reduce inaccuracies.

Training Techniques and Algorithms

The effectiveness of neural networks is amplified by various training techniques and optimization algorithms:

- **Backpropagation**: This feedback mechanism calculates errors between predicted and actual outputs, modifying connection weights accordingly to minimize discrepancies.
- **Gradient Descent**: This optimization strategy helps adjust model weights efficiently by calculating gradients for each weight, informing the system on how to reduce errors.
- **Stochastic Gradient Descent (SGD)**: In contrast to traditional gradient descent, SGD randomly selects subsets of data for each iteration, which reduces computational load while maintaining high accuracy.

These techniques are foundational for training AI models. They enhance the network's ability to recognize patterns, make accurate predictions, and refine its performance, thus advancing the capabilities of sophisticated AI systems.

Real-World Applications of Trained AI Models

As various industries harness trained AI models, transformative changes are evident:

- **Healthcare**: AI models trained on extensive medical datasets improve diagnostic accuracy and facilitate early disease detection through image analysis.
- **Financial Services**: In banking, AI algorithms are deployed to identify fraudulent transactions rapidly, enhancing security and customer trust.
- **Transportation**: AI powers self-driving vehicles, enabling them to navigate roads effectively. Moreover, logistics companies employ AI systems for optimizing delivery routes based on various factors, thus improving efficiency.

Ultimately, the breadth of applications for trained AI models reinforces their significance in modern society.

Conclusion

The journey through the landscape of machine learning elucidates the intricacies of how AI learns from data and improves continuously. Its three core methodologies—supervised learning, unsupervised learning, and reinforcement learning—delineate distinct paths through which AI can discover patterns and enhance capabilities.

Real-world applications across various sectors illustrate the profound impact AI is having on our daily lives. Whether optimizing healthcare outcomes or enhancing decision-making processes in businesses, the multilayered capabilities of AI are reshaping industries and improving outcomes.

As AI technology continues to advance, the ethical considerations surrounding its development and deployment must remain at the forefront of discussions. A careful balance between leveraging AI for innovation and addressing the consequences of its use is essential for fostering a sustainable future.

By gaining an understanding of how AI systems learn and evolve, we can better appreciate the possibilities that lie ahead—embracing the innovations while remaining vigilant about their implications for society.

CHAPTER 6: NATURAL LANGUAGE PROCESSING

Understanding and Processing Human Language

Human language is a fascinating and complex system that we often take for granted. Each day, we engage in conversations that demonstrate our innate ability to understand and interpret nuances, emotions, and cultural references within spoken or written communication. Yet, when trying to comprehend how artificial intelligence (AI) operates within this intricate framework, many questions arise. This chapter seeks to demystify the mechanisms behind AI's interaction with human language by exploring the foundational principles of natural language processing (NLP) and the role of machine learning in this dynamic field.

Key Takeaways

- AI systems can effectively understand and interpret human language.
- Machine learning is paramount in AI language processing, enabling systems to learn and improve from vast amounts of data.
- Various natural language processing techniques enhance machine learning to better understand and process human language.
- AI systems strive to effectively interpret contextual meanings and generate human-like responses to facilitate seamless communication between technology and people.

The Complexity of Human Language

Human language embodies an array of complexities. It is not merely a collection of words; it incorporates grammar, tone, context, and cultural nuances that enrich communication. For AI systems to effectively process human language, they must navigate these layers of complexity.

One primary challenge in understanding human communication lies in the inherent ambiguity of language. Words often possess multiple meanings based on surrounding context; for instance, the word "bank" can denote a financial institution or the side of a river. Additionally, context significantly influences interpretation, as evident in the phrase "I saw her duck," where the word "duck" could signify a bird or an action.

Furthermore, language is not static; it evolves, with new words and meanings emerging and slang frequently changing over time. To remain effective, AI systems must adapt to this evolving landscape through continuous training on expansive datasets that capture the nuances of linguistic change.

A profound understanding of these complexities emphasizes the critical involvement of machine learning in AI language processing. This technology allows AI systems to recognize patterns within substantial data volumes, improving over time and enhancing their language understanding capabilities. As we explore further, we will uncover the specific ways in which machine learning aids AI in tackling the intricacies of human language.

Machine Learning in AI Language Processing

Machine learning employs algorithms designed to learn from data by recognizing patterns without needing explicit programming. This ability has transformed how AI systems engage with language, enabling them to analyze human speech and text more effectively.

In language processing, machine learning algorithms analyze vast datasets, learning relationships among words and phrases within different contexts. Training on these datasets allows AI models to make predictions and understand language intricately. As these systems process more data, they receive continuous feedback, allowing them to refine their capabilities and enhance communication accuracy.

The diversity of training data is pivotal. A machine learning model trained on ample and varied content can better handle discrepancies in language use across different contexts and cultures. Additionally, machine learning equips AI systems to address the inherent ambiguity present in human communication. Through extensive exposure to examples in training, these algorithms can recognize nuanced expressions such as sarcasm and idioms, thus improving their interpretation of complex language constructs.

Having established an understanding of how machine learning bolsters AI language processing, we will now explore the natural language processing techniques that seamlessly complement these algorithms.

Natural Language Processing Techniques

Natural language processing encompasses various sophisticated techniques empowering AI systems to comprehend and manipulate human language. Here are four remarkable capabilities within NLP:

- **Sentiment Analysis**: NLP algorithms discern the sentiment or emotional tone underlying specific text segments—whether positive, negative, or neutral. This application is invaluable for businesses seeking to gauge customer attitudes toward products or services, enabling them to anticipate feedback and address concerns effectively.
- **Named Entity Recognition**: This technique analyzes text to identify and classify specific entities, including names of people, organizations, locations, and dates. Such identification allows for valuable data extraction from extensive unstructured information.
- **Text Summarization**: AI systems capable of summarizing extended texts can provide concise versions while preserving critical ideas and key points. This capability aids users in rapidly processing large volumes of information and efficiently understanding main concepts.
- **Machine Translation**: NLP empowers AI to facilitate communication between different languages through automatic translation. This technology diminishes language barriers, allowing for smoother interaction between individuals from varying linguistic backgrounds.

These NLP techniques collectively enhance the bridging of communication gaps between AI systems and human language. By harnessing their capabilities, we inch closer to developing AI that can genuinely comprehend human language's complexity and subtleties without compromising context or meaning.

Bridging the Gap Between AI and Human Language

Harnessing natural language processing techniques allows AI systems to bridge the chasm between human communication and technological capability. Powerful algorithms paired with robust machine learning models enable these systems to analyze and understand human language in increasingly sophisticated ways.

A key aspect of this bridging endeavor is contextual interpretation. Human language often relies on context to convey meaning, and AI systems are now equipped to analyze words within their surrounding environments, enabling them to discern nuances such as sarcasm and irony that can be present in both spoken and written language.

Another critical asset is the capability to generate human-like responses. By fusing deep learning techniques with extensive datasets, AI systems can not only comprehend user input but also formulate sentences that mirror natural human speech patterns. This interplay enhances the overall communication experience, fostering more intuitive interactions.

Advancements in AI technology have led to increasingly natural interactions with machines—whether through virtual assistants executing voice commands or chatbots providing customer support. As these capacities continue to evolve, we move closer to a future characterized by seamless human-machine communication and engagement.

Demystifying AI Language Processing

AI systems generate responses that resonate with natural human interaction, leveraging sophisticated natural language processing algorithms to understand and contextualize spoken and written words. These algorithms break down human language into manageable components, allowing for improved comprehension.

A widely utilized method in this endeavor is machine learning, which relies on extensive data exposure to recognize patterns and formulate predictions regarding human responses. For example, a chatbot may train on numerous conversations to identify typical responses associated with particular user inputs. Through this iterative learning process, AI systems refine their understanding and improve their ability to engage users effectively.

To further enhance comprehension, developers address challenges such as ambiguity and context within human language. Ambiguous phrases can have multiple interpretations depending on surrounding context. To mitigate these confounding aspects, developers employ techniques like word embeddings, which numerically represent words based on contextual usage within large datasets.

Utilizing these technologies fosters a remarkable synergy between human language processing and AI systems. Each conversation with a digital assistant or chatbot brings forward a network of algorithms tailored to replicate human communication patterns.

Frequently Asked Questions

How does AI language processing handle the nuances and complexities of human language?

AI language processing employs advanced algorithms to analyze grammar, context, and semantics for accurate meaning interpretation. This ability allows AI to produce suitable responses during real-time conversations.

What are some common challenges faced by AI language processing systems?
AI language processing systems frequently encounter hurdles related to ambiguity, sarcasm, cultural references, and idiomatic expressions, complicating the task of decoding linguistic intricacies.

Can AI language processing systems understand informal or slang language?
Yes, advanced algorithms enable AI language processing systems to analyze patterns and contexts, facilitating the comprehension of informal language and slang.

How does machine learning improve AI language processing capabilities?
Machine learning refines AI language processing through continuous training on extensive data, empowering algorithms to recognize patterns, understand context, and enhance accuracy.

What ethical considerations arise with AI language processing technology?
Ethical concerns include privacy issues, inherent algorithm biases, implications for job displacement, and the potential misuse of AI technology for propaganda or manipulation.

Conclusion

The intricate tapestry of human language and AI advances in language processing presents a captivating intersection. Through the foundation laid by machine learning, AI has become a formidable tool in shedding light on the complexities embedded within our words.

By exploring natural language processing techniques and bridging the chasm between human interaction and technology, AI serves as an invaluable resource in deciphering our intricate conversational structures. Through diligent research and innovative algorithm development, AI systems have progressed in understanding context, nuance, and emotion in communication, enabling more succinct interaction possibilities.

With our progressive curiosity and continued technological advancements, we stand on the precipice of a future where communication between humans and machines is fluid, fostering unparalleled advancements across fields including healthcare, education, and customer service. AI's influence will play a pivotal role in a world where language barriers dissolve, enhancing interpersonal relations and shaping our collective future.

Text Analysis and Sentiment Analysis

Text analysis serves to investigate written or spoken language, extracting insights that inform decision-making and enhance understanding. When coupled with sentiment analysis—the ability to gauge emotions and opinions expressed within text—these tools help synthesize large volumes of content efficiently.

The Functionality of Text Analysis and Sentiment Analysis

Text analysis algorithms are designed to process vast quantities of information, uncovering key themes and patterns across various types of text, including emails, online reviews, and social media posts. This functionality allows us to derive valuable insights without needing to sift through every line manually. Applications include brand monitoring and social listening, improving customer relationships by enabling data-driven decisions.

Sentiment analysis focuses specifically on detecting the emotional tone behind written expressions. This technology is particularly beneficial across industries, allowing businesses to analyze customer opinions regarding products or services through feedback channels. Equipped with sentiment tools, organizations can actively manage customer engagement and address emerging issues.

Key Takeaways

- Sentiment analysis aids businesses in monitoring feedback and addressing potential issues proactively.
- AI-driven text analysis provides insights into customer preferences, facilitating informed decisions and improvements based on feedback.
- Text analysis is essential for risk management and fraud detection, identifying patterns and anomalies within textual data.
- AI enhances reputation management by proactively addressing sentiments before they escalate.

Exploring Text Analysis and its Applications

Text analysis leverages AI to decipher the meaning behind written words, illuminating the intricate layers embedded in the text. By analyzing structure, identifying patterns, and extracting vital information, AI can unveil sentiments, emotions, and themes.

Applications of text analysis are integral in our everyday lives. For instance, businesses can utilize text analysis tools to comprehend customer feedback from reviews and social media, enabling them to recognize satisfaction levels and improve service offerings. Similarly, text analysis supports public sentiment monitoring regarding political campaigns or societal issues.

Practical Applications of Text Analysis

Here are several impactful applications of text analysis in recent times:

- **Customer Feedback Analysis**: AI-algorithms help businesses analyze extensive volumes of customer feedback from various platforms, leading to improved understanding and enhanced product offerings.
- **Content Moderation**: Platforms utilize text analysis to moderate user-generated content, ensuring compliance and safety within communities by identifying inappropriate language.
- **Market Research**: Researchers analyze textual data from sources like blogs or social media to derive consumer insights and market trends, aiding strategic decision-making in business.
- **Personalized Recommendations**: Streaming services use text analysis to recommend tailored content based on user behavior, enhancing the overall user experience.

Text analysis harnesses the power of AI technologies, unveiling the ability to comprehend not only what is being said but also the underlying feelings. This capability allows organizations to gain invaluable insight into public sentiment across various domains, all without directly querying individuals about their thoughts or emotions.

The Power of Sentiment Analysis

Sentiment analysis enables the deciphering of emotions and drives informed decision-making. By analyzing opinions, attitudes, and sentiments in text, businesses can empower better brand management and customer insights.

One major application is brand reputation management. Through sentiment monitoring, companies can detect and address negative feedback before it escalates, reinforcing proactive strategies and showcasing responsive brand identity. Additionally, sentiment analysis assists in market research, allowing businesses to gauge their products' reception and tailor decisions to bolster market success.

The Impacts of AI-Powered Text Analysis

AI-powered text analysis may appear to be a common term, yet its impact is profoundly felt in everyday decision-making. With comprehensive text data analysis, organizations can glean insights into customer preferences and sentiment, enabling informed strategies to enhance engagement and satisfaction.

Sentiment analysis extends its utility into risk management and fraud detection. AI algorithms can analyze communications across various sources, such as emails, flagging suspicious activities or potential risks. Businesses can employ these insights to preemptively protect themselves from fraudulent behaviors.

Furthermore, the role of AI in reputation management empowers both businesses and individuals to monitor evolving public sentiment. By analyzing social media and news, one can take strategic actions based on real-time public perception feedback, positively influencing how they are viewed.

In summary, AI-powered text analysis revolutionizes decision-making processes across industries, transforming our understanding of written communication.

Frequently Asked Questions

How does artificial intelligence (AI) work in text analysis?

AI employs algorithms to extract meaning from text by identifying patterns, keywords, and sentiments to generate insights and predictions about content.

Can text analysis combat cyberbullying?

Yes, text analysis can detect harmful behaviors in online content, identifying patterns associated with cyberbullying, thus allowing for prompt remedial action.

Is sentiment analysis confined to marketing?

Sentiment analysis transcends marketing, applicable to diverse sectors such as customer service, political analysis, and healthcare, helping understand emotions across various contexts.

What ethical concerns arise regarding AI-powered text analysis?

Ethical concerns include biases, potential privacy breaches, accountability issues, and the implications of automated analyses on autonomous decision-making.

Are there challenges in implementing AI-powered text analysis?

Yes, challenges include attaining accuracy, managing bias and privacy concerns, and continuous updates to keep pace with shifting language and context.

Conclusion

The exploration of AI capabilities in text analysis and sentiment analysis grants us significant insight into their transformative potential. AI-driven algorithms are adept at analyzing vast text datasets, enabling intelligent insights across diverse industries.

While an estimated 80% of today's data is unstructured text, AI facilitates understanding, allowing organizations to distill relevance from the digital noise. Sentiment analysis shines in this process, enabling companies to align their strategies with genuine consumer feedback.

As AI technology continues to evolve rapidly, the possibilities for text and sentiment analysis expand, reshaping our comprehension of user experiences and enhancing engagement across various domains.

Speech Recognition and Synthesis

Speech recognition represents technology allowing computers to interpret human speech, converting spoken words into text. Using machine learning, these advanced systems listen to spoken input, decipher meanings, and respond appropriately, fundamentally transforming human-technology interaction.

The Power Behind Speech Recognition

Speech recognition technology has revolutionized our relationship with devices. Users today can dictate messages, inquire about information, or control smart home devices merely through voice commands.

Central to this technology's success is the ability of AI to capture and analyze spoken words effectively. Sophisticated algorithms match sound waves generated by the user's voice against expansive datasets of voice samples to identify words accurately. Training on diverse data equips these algorithms to handle various accents, languages, and background noises, enabling a seamless interaction.

As these systems ingest expansive audio recordings paired with transcriptions, they analyze speech patterns, transitioning from phonemes to recognizing complete phrases. Through deep learning mechanisms, these models dissect visual representations of sound spectrograms, identifying similarities and extracting meaningful features.

The conjunction of data analysis, pattern recognition, and machine learning allows AI to decode spoken communication while facilitating a smoother interaction.

Transforming Text into Natural-Sounding Speech

The advancement of technology allows for a unique experience where written text is translated into natural-sounding speech. This process involves several sequential steps.

First, the machine analyzes the structural components of the text. Next, linguistic rules for pronunciation—considering context and emphasis—are applied. Finally, using sophisticated algorithms, a corresponding speech waveform is generated that reflects intonation and rhythm akin to human speech.

Two primary methodologies underlie speech synthesis:

- **Concatenative Synthesis**: Involves piecing together pre-recorded snippets of human speech to form coherent sentences. This technique tailors speech outputs by blending recorded snippets, resulting in lifelike voice generation.
- **Parametric Synthesis**: Utilizes mathematical models to generate speech waveforms by controlling parameters like pitch and duration. Although offering flexibility in voice creation, this approach requires significant training on diverse datasets.

AI-driven speech technology profoundly impacts various sectors, enhancing accessibility for individuals with disabilities and streamlining customer service interactions through advanced voice-command capabilities.

The Impact of AI-Powered Speech Technology

AI-powered speech technology facilitates effortless communication with devices like virtual assistants. The ability to utilize voice commands has reshaped our engagement with technology, enhancing convenience and productivity.

AI-driven speech recognition optimizes user experiences, especially for individuals with disabilities. For example, a visually impaired individual can navigate smart devices through voice commands, promoting independence and accessibility.

The customer service industry benefits significantly from AI speech technology, which deploys chatbots to provide real-time assistance, improving customer satisfaction while reducing organizational costs.

The capacity for machines to produce high-quality synthesized speech enhances productivity by automating repetitive tasks in creative fields like entertainment, where realistic digital voices replace human actors for certain roles.

Frequently Asked Questions

How does AI utilize speech recognition to decode human speech?
AI leverages speech recognition by analyzing vocal input, converting it into text, and subsequently processing the text to understand its meaning.

What challenges exist when converting text into natural-sounding speech?
Key challenges include ensuring proper intonation and inflection, as well as accommodating language and accent variations.

Can AI technology accommodate multiple languages in speech processing?
Yes, AI is adaptable, recognizing and generating speech across various languages, addressing diverse linguistic needs.

In what ways can AI-powered speech technology revolutionize industries?
Speech technology can enhance customer service through automated inquiries, content creation, and interactive voice systems.

How does AI-powered speech recognition compare to traditional processing methods?
AI methods exceed traditional processing through machine learning capabilities that enhance understanding and provide faster, more refined communication.

Conclusion

Through an exploration of AI's capabilities in speech recognition and synthesis, one can appreciate the extraordinary potential of machine intelligence in current communication dynamics. Imagine effortlessly speaking to your devices: asking your AI to navigate the nearest gas station while driving seamlessly highlights the benefits of speech recognition and synthesis.

As AI technology continues to advance, we can anticipate new breakthroughs in the realm of oral communication, optimizing our interactions with technology while bridging cultural and linguistic gaps.

Machine Translation and Language Generation

In a globalized society, the ability to communicate across languages is vital. Machine translation harnesses AI to facilitate this communication, automatically translating text or speech from one language to another. This technology has forever transformed our connections with diverse cultures, fostering international dialogue.

Understanding Machine Translation

Machine translation employs AI algorithms to ensure that understanding transcends linguistic barriers. It provides real-time translation, allowing individuals to communicate effortlessly with those who speak different languages. This capability has been pivotal for businesses seeking international expansion while also playing a crucial role in humanitarian efforts during emergencies.

By utilizing machine translation, organizations can cater to a wider audience, leveraging global markets and enhancing customer relations. Furthermore, this technology supports cultural exchange by allowing access to literature, film, and art in their original languages, enhancing cultural appreciation.

Challenges and Ethical Considerations

Despite its advantages, machine translation faces numerous challenges. Achieving accuracy remains a primary concern, as languages possess varying structures and idiomatic expressions. Additionally, ethical considerations can limit the use of AI in translation. Issues such as bias and misinformation must be continuously addressed to ensure responsible deployment.

The balancing act involves providing effective translations without oversimplifying nuances or contributing to linguistic discrimination. Developers must constantly refine and assess AI's handling of context while prioritizing ethical standards.

Language Generation: The Power of AI Writing

Language generation utilizes AI to produce human-like text based on given prompts. This capability unlocks novel possibilities—automating content creation, forming personalized messaging systems, and even aiding in creative storytelling.

AI writing tools allow businesses to enhance their communication effectively. From drafting social media posts to generating marketing materials, the efficiency gained through language generation can accelerate productivity across sectors.

Moreover, AI's writing tools can cater to individual preferences, thus improving personal expression. As AI operates risks involving misinformation, ongoing oversight is fundamental to uphold standards and ensure responsible deployment.

Challenges and Future Possibilities

Looking forward, significant hurdles persist. Accuracy in translation and contextual understanding are paramount challenges still facing developers. Additionally, concerns over plagiarism and automation misuse warrant ongoing reflection.

On a positive note, the future of language generation holds promise for personalized solutions catering to individual writing styles, ultimately transforming how communities produce and consume content.

Frequently Asked Questions

What ethical concerns emerge with machine translation and language generation?
Key concerns include potential biases in translation, job displacement, issues of plagiarism, and the risk of misinformation.

How does AI handle complex idiomatic expressions?
AI analyzes the contextual meanings behind idioms, refining translations that maintain the underlying message.

Can AI-generated language replicate emotional nuances?
AI has made strides in mimicking emotional language; however, there remain limitations, particularly concerning contextual and cultural understanding.

What measures are employed to ensure user privacy in AI writing tools?
Common measures include employing encryption, anonymization, user consent protocols, and adherence to privacy regulations.

Are challenges present in translating languages with divergent grammatical structures?
Yes, translating between languages with vastly different structures poses difficulties in accurately capturing linguistic nuances and cultural contexts.

Conclusion

In conclusion, the exploration of AI's role in language translation and generation reveals its transformative power in fostering communication. Machine translation helps us overcome language barriers, enabling a fluid exchange of ideas and cultural appreciation.

Moreover, AI's capacity for generating coherent language transforms content creation. However, addressing challenges related to accuracy, context, and ethical implementation remains vital for AI's responsible evolution.

The future brims with potential as technology continues to advance, promising a world where communication is unbound—uniting communities across languages and cultures. The promise of AI within our global narrative is one of growth, understanding, and connection.

CHAPTER 7: BASICS OF COMPUTER VISION AND IMAGE PROCESSING

Computer vision is the field of AI that focuses on teaching computers to analyze and understand visual data, just like our human eyes do. By leveraging algorithms and mathematical models, machines can detect patterns, recognize objects or faces, extract features from images, and even perform complex tasks such as object tracking or gesture recognition. It's like giving them a pair of electronic eyes that see beyond what meets the human eye!

Key Takeaways

- Computer vision is a field that focuses on teaching computers to understand and analyze visual data.
- It involves algorithms and mathematical models to detect patterns, recognize objects, and extract features from images.
- Computer vision works by breaking down images into pixels and analyzing patterns and shapes.
- Image processing enhances image quality and extracts specific features to make intelligent decisions based on visual input.

Understanding Computer Vision and Image Processing

Imagine yourself standing in front of a computer screen, watching as the magic of computer vision and image processing unfolds before your eyes. Computer vision is the field that focuses on teaching computers to see and understand the world just like humans do. It involves analyzing and interpreting digital images or videos to extract meaningful information from them.

Image processing, on the other hand, deals with manipulating images to enhance their quality or extract specific features. Computer vision and image processing work together seamlessly to enable machines to recognize objects, detect patterns, and make intelligent decisions based on visual input. For example, imagine a self-driving car using computer vision algorithms to identify pedestrians, traffic signs, and other vehicles on the road. These technologies rely on complex algorithms that process vast amounts of data in real-time.

Now let's dive into how computer vision works without getting too technical. By breaking down an image into pixels (individual units of color), a computer can analyze patterns and shapes within it. This process involves several steps such as edge detection, segmentation, feature extraction, and object recognition. Each step contributes to building a comprehensive understanding of what is being seen in the image.

Without realizing it, you've already witnessed some aspects of computer vision in action - think about face detection technology used in smartphone cameras or social media platforms tagging people automatically. So next time you come across an amazing photo app filter or marvel at autonomous vehicles navigating through busy streets effortlessly, remember that behind all this lies the power of artificial intelligence combined with the basics of computer vision and image processing.

How Computer Vision Works

By using advanced algorithms and cutting-edge technology, Computer Vision has the ability to decipher visual information like a detective piecing together clues at a crime scene. It takes in digital images or video frames and analyzes them to understand and interpret what's being seen.

Here's how it works:

- Feature detection: Computer Vision starts by identifying key features in an image, such as edges, corners, or color blobs. These features act as building blocks for further analysis.

- Image segmentation: The next step involves dividing the image into meaningful regions based on similarities in color, texture, or shape. This helps separate objects from their backgrounds and enables more focused processing.

- Object recognition: Once the image is segmented, Computer Vision compares the identified regions with previously learned patterns or models to recognize specific objects or categories. This involves matching against a database of known images or using machine learning techniques.

- Motion tracking: In video processing, Computer Vision can track moving objects across frames by analyzing their motion patterns. This allows for applications like object tracking in surveillance videos or gesture recognition in gaming.

- 3D reconstruction: Using multiple images from different viewpoints, Computer Vision can reconstruct a three-dimensional representation of the scene. This is useful for applications like virtual reality simulations and autonomous navigation.

With its ability to analyze visual data and make sense of it, computer vision finds applications in various aspects of our everyday lives. From facial recognition on smartphones to self-driving cars navigating through traffic, computer vision plays a vital role in many modern technologies. Its potential goes beyond convenience; it can also assist doctors in medical diagnoses or help monitor manufacturing processes for quality control purposes.

Understanding how computer vision works sets the foundation for exploring these exciting applications that are shaping our world today.

Applications of Computer Vision in Everyday Life

Explore the numerous ways computer vision impacts your daily life, from recognizing faces on social media to assisting in autonomous vehicles.

Computer vision technology is used in various applications that we encounter every day. For instance, when you upload a photo on social media and it automatically suggests tagging your friends, that's computer vision at work. It can recognize faces by analyzing different facial features such as eyes, nose, and mouth.

Computer vision also plays a significant role in enhancing security systems. Many surveillance cameras use this technology to identify potential threats or suspicious activities in real-time. This helps law enforcement agencies keep public spaces safe and secure.

Additionally, computer vision is utilized in medical imaging to aid doctors in diagnosing diseases accurately and efficiently.

Computer vision has become an integral part of our everyday lives through its applications such as face recognition on social media platforms and enhancing security measures with surveillance cameras. It also contributes to the field of medicine by assisting doctors in diagnosing diseases effectively.

The next section will delve into the role of artificial intelligence (AI) in enabling computer vision algorithms to perform these tasks seamlessly without human intervention.

The Role of AI in Computer Vision

Artificial intelligence enhances computer vision capabilities, allowing it to accurately analyze and interpret visual data for various applications in our daily lives. Here are three ways AI plays a crucial role in computer vision:

- Object Recognition: AI algorithms enable computers to identify and categorize objects within images or videos. By training deep learning models on vast datasets, AI can recognize not only common objects but also complex ones with high accuracy. This technology has practical applications such as facial recognition in smartphones, automated surveillance systems that detect suspicious activities, and even self-driving cars that can perceive their surroundings.

- Image Segmentation: With the help of AI, computer vision can divide an image into different segments based on its content. This segmentation allows us to extract specific information from the image and understand the relationships between different elements within it. For example, medical professionals use this technique to analyze MRI scans by segmenting organs or tumors for accurate diagnosis.

- Scene Understanding: By combining computer vision with AI techniques like machine learning and natural language processing, computers can gain a deeper understanding of what's happening within an image or video. They can infer the context, identify actions being performed, and even generate textual descriptions of scenes automatically. This advancement has implications in areas like autonomous robotics, where machines need to comprehend their environment to perform tasks effectively.

As we delve deeper into the implications and future developments of computer vision technology, it's essential to highlight how artificial intelligence continues to push its boundaries further than ever before.

Implications and Future Developments of Computer Vision Technology

One fascinating statistic to consider is that the global market for computer vision technology is projected to reach $48.32 billion by 2023, indicating its immense potential and future growth prospects.

The implications of this technology are far-reaching and have the potential to revolutionize various industries. One area where computer vision is already making a significant impact is in healthcare. With advanced image processing algorithms, doctors can now analyze medical images more accurately and efficiently, leading to better diagnoses and treatment plans.

Another important implication of computer vision technology is in the field of autonomous vehicles. Self-driving cars heavily rely on computer vision systems to perceive their surroundings and make decisions accordingly. These systems use cameras, sensors, and deep learning algorithms to detect objects, read road signs, and navigate through complex traffic situations. As this technology continues to improve, we can expect safer roads with fewer accidents caused by human error.

Looking ahead, there are exciting developments on the horizon for computer vision. One area that holds great promise is augmented reality (AR) and virtual reality (VR). Computer vision plays a crucial role in creating immersive experiences by overlaying digital information onto real-world environments or creating entirely virtual worlds. This technology has already found applications in gaming and entertainment but has the potential for much broader use cases such as training simulations, remote collaboration, and architectural design.

The current projections for the global market of computer vision technology highlight its immense potential for growth. Its implications in healthcare, autonomous vehicles, augmented reality/virtual reality demonstrate how it can revolutionize various industries. As advancements continue to be made in this field, we can expect even more exciting developments that will shape our future in ways we may not yet fully comprehend.

Frequently Asked Questions

Are there any limitations to computer vision and image processing technology?
Yes, there are limitations to computer vision and image processing technology. It may struggle with complex scenes or objects, low-quality images, and variations in lighting. Additionally, it can be challenging to achieve real-time processing and accurate object recognition.

How does computer vision technology differentiate between objects with similar appearances?
Computer vision technology differentiates between objects with similar appearances by analyzing their unique features, like color, shape, and texture. It uses advanced algorithms to extract these distinguishing characteristics, enabling it to make accurate distinctions.

Can computer vision technology be used to recognize emotions or facial expressions?
Yes, computer vision technology can be used to recognize emotions and facial expressions. It analyzes various facial features like eyes, mouth, and eyebrows to determine emotions such as happiness, sadness, or anger.

What are the ethical concerns surrounding the use of computer vision technology in surveillance systems?
The ethical concerns surrounding computer vision technology in surveillance systems involve issues of privacy, civil liberties, and potential abuse. It's important to carefully consider the balance between security and personal freedoms when implementing these technologies.

Are there any potential risks or dangers associated with the widespread implementation of computer vision technology in various industries?
There are potential risks and dangers associated with the widespread implementation of computer vision technology in various industries. These include privacy concerns, biases in algorithms, and the potential for misuse or abuse of the technology.

Conclusion

In conclusion, you've embarked on a journey to unravel the mysteries of computer vision and image processing. Like a skilled artist, you've learned how computers can perceive and interpret the visual world around us. Through this newfound knowledge, you now understand the immense potential of computer vision in various aspects of our everyday lives.

Just as a master painter brings life to a canvas with every stroke of their brush, AI breathes life into computer vision technology. With its ability to learn and adapt, AI acts as the guiding hand that enhances the capabilities of computer systems. It empowers machines to analyze images with remarkable accuracy and efficiency, opening doors to countless applications that were once mere figments of imagination.

As you move forward, keep in mind that the realm of computer vision is ever-evolving. Just like an enchanting kaleidoscope constantly changing its patterns, new developments in this field promise exciting possibilities for the future. From self-driving cars navigating bustling city streets to medical diagnoses reaching unprecedented levels of accuracy - brace yourself for a world where computers see, understand, and interact with our visual reality like never before.

So go forth armed with your newfound understanding! Embrace this fusion of artistry and technology as you delve deeper into the mesmerizing world of computer vision and image processing. And just like an artist who unveils breathtaking masterpieces one brushstroke at a time, may you uncover new insights and create innovative solutions that shape our future in ways we can only dream about today.

Object Detection and Recognition

Artificial intelligence, or AI for short, refers to the ability of machines to perform tasks that typically require human intelligence. Object detection is a fundamental aspect of AI that involves teaching machines to identify and locate specific objects within images or videos. It works by analyzing patterns and features within visual data, such as colors, shapes, and textures. Through advanced algorithms, AI systems are able to accurately pinpoint various objects in a given scene.

Once an object is detected, recognition comes into play – this is where the AI system is trained to classify the object into specific categories or even identify individuals based on their unique characteristics. The combination of object detection and recognition enables machines to understand their surroundings and interact with them in meaningful ways.

Whether it's identifying faces in photos on social media platforms or detecting potential hazards on the road for autonomous vehicles, object detection and recognition have become essential tools for AI applications across various industries.

Key Takeaways
- AI and object detection have the potential to revolutionize various industries.
- Smart shelves in grocery stores can automatically detect low stock and restock themselves.
- AI-powered object recognition can assist doctors during surgeries, providing real-time information about vital signs, organ structures, and anomalies.
- Object detection technology can make self-driving cars safer and more reliable by recognizing pedestrians, traffic signals, road signs, and other vehicles.

The Basics of Artificial Intelligence

Artificial intelligence works by using algorithms and mathematical models to analyze large amounts of data. This data can come in different forms, such as images, text, or sensor readings. The algorithms then learn from this data and make predictions or take actions based on what they have learned.

In the case of object detection and recognition, AI algorithms are trained on image datasets that contain labeled examples of different objects. They learn to identify patterns and features in these images that correspond to specific objects.

AI algorithms use a variety of techniques for object detection and recognition. One common approach is called deep learning, which involves training neural networks with many layers to recognize patterns in images. These neural networks are inspired by the structure of the human brain and can learn complex relationships between pixels in an image. By analyzing different layers of the network, AI algorithms can detect objects at various levels of detail.

Now that you understand the basics of artificial intelligence and how it learns from data to perform tasks like object detection and recognition, let's dive deeper into how exactly object detection works.

How Object Detection Works

Additionally, did you know that object detection algorithms can identify and locate multiple objects in an image with an impressive accuracy rate of up to 90%? This remarkable capability is achieved through a combination of advanced techniques and machine learning.

Here's a closer look at how object detection works:

- **Feature Extraction**: The first step in object detection is extracting relevant features from the image. These features can be edges, corners, textures, or even more complex patterns. By analyzing these features, the algorithm creates a representation of the objects present in the image.

- **Classification**: Once the features are extracted, the algorithm uses them to classify different parts of the image as either objects or background. It compares these features with a pre-trained model that has learned patterns from vast amounts of labeled data. This allows it to make accurate predictions about what objects are present in the image.

- **Localization**: After classifying the objects, the algorithm goes one step further by localizing them within the image. It does this by drawing bounding boxes around each identified object to indicate their position and size accurately.

With these steps combined, object detection algorithms can not only recognize various objects but also pinpoint their location within an image. This technology has numerous practical applications across various fields like autonomous vehicles, surveillance systems, and even medical diagnostics.

Now let's delve into why recognition plays a crucial role in artificial intelligence research and development...

The Importance of Recognition in AI

Imagine being able to witness the extraordinary power of AI as it effortlessly identifies and understands the world around you. Recognition is a vital aspect of AI, as it allows machines to not only detect objects but also classify and understand them. By recognizing objects, AI systems can differentiate between various entities and assign meaning to them.

This capability enables AI to comprehend visual data in a way that was once exclusive to humans.

Recognition plays a crucial role in enabling AI systems to interact with their surroundings effectively. For instance, in autonomous vehicles, object recognition allows the vehicle's system to identify traffic signs, pedestrians, and other vehicles on the road. This information then helps the vehicle make informed decisions about its actions, such as stopping at red lights or avoiding obstacles. Without recognition capabilities, AI would be limited to basic detection without any understanding of the context or significance of the objects it detects.

Recognition is an essential component of AI that elevates its abilities beyond mere object detection. It empowers AI systems with comprehension and understanding of their environment by assigning meaning to detected objects. With recognition, AI becomes capable of interacting with the real world in ways that were previously unimaginable.

Now let's explore some real-world applications where object detection and recognition are revolutionizing various industries without skipping a beat!

Real-World Applications of Object Detection and Recognition

Unleashing the power of advanced technology, industries are witnessing a remarkable transformation as machines effortlessly perceive and understand their surroundings, forever changing the way we live and work.

Object detection and recognition have found their way into countless real-world applications, revolutionizing various fields. One area where these technologies excel is in autonomous vehicles. Through object detection and recognition, self-driving cars can accurately identify pedestrians, traffic lights, and other vehicles on the road, enabling them to navigate safely and efficiently. This not only enhances road safety but also opens up possibilities for streamlined transportation systems.

Another realm where object detection and recognition play a crucial role is in surveillance systems. By utilizing AI algorithms to detect objects of interest in real-time video footage or images, security cameras can automatically alert authorities about potential threats or suspicious activities. This not only saves time but also ensures a swift response to prevent any untoward incidents.

Additionally, retail businesses employ object recognition technology to track inventory levels on store shelves accurately. With this capability, they can quickly identify when products need restocking or if there are any misplaced items.

Object detection and recognition have made significant strides in solving real-world challenges across various industries. From improving road safety through autonomous vehicles to enhancing security with intelligent surveillance systems, these technologies continue to reshape our everyday lives for the better.

As we delve deeper into the future of AI and object detection, exciting advancements await us that will further augment our capabilities and make our world more connected than ever before. With the increasing integration of intelligent surveillance systems, we can expect a future where AI-powered object detection not only enhances our safety and security but also revolutionizes various industries such as transportation, retail, and healthcare.

These advancements will enable seamless automation, precise data analysis, and real-time decision-making, ultimately leading to improved efficiency, enhanced customer experiences, and a more interconnected global society.

The Future of AI and Object Detection

As you look ahead, envision a world where advanced technology seamlessly integrates with our daily lives, transforming the way we perceive and interact with our surroundings. The future of AI and object detection holds immense potential for revolutionizing various industries.

Imagine walking into a grocery store where smart shelves automatically detect when items are running low and restock themselves without any human intervention. This not only saves time for both customers and store employees but also ensures that the shelves are always well-stocked.

Moreover, in the field of healthcare, AI-powered object recognition can play a crucial role in assisting doctors during surgeries. Imagine surgeons having access to real-time information about the patient's vital signs, organ structures, and potential anomalies through augmented reality glasses or heads-up displays. This would enable them to make quicker and more accurate decisions, ultimately leading to better patient outcomes.

Another exciting aspect is the use of AI in transportation. With advancements in object detection technology, self-driving cars will become safer and more reliable on our roads. These vehicles will be able to recognize pedestrians, traffic signals, road signs, and other vehicles with precision. By eliminating human error from driving equations, accidents caused by distracted driving or fatigue could be significantly reduced.

As we peer into the future of AI and object detection technology, it becomes evident that its impact will extend far beyond what we can currently imagine. From streamlining everyday tasks to enhancing medical procedures and improving transportation safety measures – the possibilities are endless. Embracing this transformative power will undoubtedly pave the way for a smarter world that prioritizes efficiency, accuracy, and convenience in all aspects of life.

Frequently Asked Questions

How does artificial intelligence impact other industries apart from object detection and recognition?
Artificial intelligence has a significant impact on various industries beyond object detection and recognition. It improves efficiency, automates tasks, enhances decision-making, and revolutionizes healthcare, finance, transportation, customer service, and many other sectors.

Are there any limitations or challenges in object detection and recognition that AI technology is yet to overcome?
Yes, there are limitations and challenges in object detection and recognition that AI technology is yet to overcome. These include issues with accuracy, handling occlusions and variations in lighting conditions, and the need for large amounts of labeled data for training.

Can object detection and recognition be used for security purposes?
Yes, object detection and recognition can be used for security purposes. It allows for the identification of potential threats or suspicious activities in real-time, enhancing surveillance systems and aiding in crime prevention.

What are the potential ethical concerns surrounding AI and object detection technology?
Ethical concerns surrounding AI and object detection technology include invasion of privacy, potential biases in data, and the risk of misuse for surveillance or discrimination. These issues raise important questions about safeguards and responsible use of this powerful technology.

How does AI technology improve the accuracy and efficiency of object detection and recognition compared to traditional methods?

AI technology improves object detection and recognition by using advanced algorithms to analyze vast amounts of data, allowing for more accurate and efficient identification of objects compared to traditional methods.

Conclusion

In conclusion, you now have a better understanding of how AI and object detection and recognition work. You've learned that AI is the technology that allows machines to perform tasks that typically require human intelligence, such as detecting and recognizing objects.

Object detection involves identifying and locating specific objects within an image or video, while recognition focuses on understanding what those objects are.

The importance of object detection and recognition in AI cannot be overstated. Just like how a sharp-eyed detective can quickly pick out important clues from a crime scene, AI-powered systems can analyze vast amounts of visual data to identify critical information. This ability has countless real-world applications, from enhancing security surveillance systems to improving self-driving cars' ability to navigate complex environments.

Looking ahead, the future of AI and object detection holds immense potential. As technology continues to advance at an unprecedented rate, we can expect even more sophisticated algorithms and models capable of accurately detecting and recognizing objects with incredible speed and precision. Imagine a world where autonomous robots can seamlessly interact with their surroundings or smart homes that anticipate your needs before you even realize them – this future isn't so far-fetched thanks to the ongoing advancements in AI.

So, remember, just like how our brains effortlessly recognize familiar faces in a crowd, AI enables machines to do the same with thousands upon thousands of images or videos – all at lightning speed! With each passing day, we inch closer towards achieving an AI-driven world where object detection and recognition become second nature for intelligent machines.

Image Classification and Segmentation

Image classification is one of the key areas where AI has made significant advancements. It involves categorizing images into different classes or categories based on their visual characteristics.

With AI-powered algorithms, computers can now analyze thousands of images quickly and accurately, enabling them to recognize objects, people, or scenes with astonishing precision. This technology has wide-ranging applications in industries such as healthcare, finance, retail, and more.

Key Takeaways

- AI-based image classification and segmentation technologies are used in various industries to analyze and interpret visual data.
- Image segmentation is used in agriculture to improve crop yield and quality by precisely mapping fields and counting plants.
- Retailers utilize image segmentation to provide personalized recommendations based on visual preferences, analyzing customer photos or browsing history to suggest outfits.
- Smart visual recognition technology enhances safety in transportation by detecting road signs, traffic lights, pedestrians, and can quickly identify suspicious activities or intruders in surveillance systems.

The Importance of Image Classification

Image classification allows AI systems to identify and sort images into different categories based on their visual features. This capability has numerous practical applications, such as organizing large collections of photos, identifying objects or scenes in real-time for autonomous vehicles, and even assisting in medical diagnostics by analyzing medical images.

By accurately classifying images, AI systems can provide valuable insights and support decision-making processes across industries.

One of the key benefits of image classification is its ability to automate tasks that would otherwise require human intervention. For example, in e-commerce, image classification can be used to automatically tag products with relevant labels or descriptions based on their appearance. This not only saves time but also improves the overall customer experience by making it easier for users to find what they're looking for.

Moreover, advancements in image segmentation have further enhanced the capabilities of AI systems when it comes to understanding visual data. Image segmentation involves dividing an image into multiple segments or regions based on certain characteristics like color, texture, or shape. This technique allows AI algorithms to precisely identify objects within an image and separate them from the background or other elements. The combination of image classification and segmentation enables AI systems to analyze complex visual data more effectively and extract meaningful information from images without human assistance.

With these advancements in image segmentation techniques, AI systems can now go beyond simply classifying images into predefined categories. They can accurately identify specific objects within an image and understand their spatial relationships within the scene. This opens up new possibilities for applications such as object detection, instance segmentation (where each individual instance of an object is identified), and even generating 3D reconstructions from 2D images.

In the subsequent section about 'advancements in image segmentation,' we'll explore how these techniques have revolutionized computer vision tasks and improved the accuracy and efficiency of AI-powered image analysis processes without relying on explicit step-by-step instructions.

Advancements in Image Segmentation

Advancements in image segmentation have revolutionized the way computers understand and analyze visual data, allowing them to accurately identify objects within an image and extract meaningful information without human intervention.

Image segmentation refers to the process of dividing an image into multiple segments or regions based on certain characteristics such as color, texture, or shape. This technique enables computers to differentiate between foreground and background elements in an image, making it easier for them to classify objects accurately.

One significant advancement in image segmentation is the use of deep learning algorithms, particularly convolutional neural networks (CNNs), which have proven to be highly effective in this task. CNNs are designed to mimic the biological processes that occur in the human brain when interpreting visual stimuli. By processing images through multiple layers of artificial neurons, CNNs can capture complex patterns and features necessary for accurate segmentation.

These advancements in image segmentation have opened up a wide range of applications across various industries. In healthcare, for example, AI-powered image segmentation allows doctors to detect abnormalities or tumors from medical scans more efficiently. In autonomous driving systems, accurate object segmentation helps vehicles recognize pedestrians, traffic signs, and other vehicles on the road. Moreover, these advancements have also found applications in fields like agriculture, retail analytics, security surveillance systems, and many more.

With such remarkable progress in image segmentation techniques driven by AI technology, computers can now interpret visual data with increasing accuracy and reliability. This has paved the way for numerous practical applications across different industries where automated analysis of images is crucial for decision-making processes.

Applications of AI in Various Industries

The implementation of artificial intelligence (AI) has revolutionized various industries by leveraging advanced algorithms to analyze visual data and make informed decisions.

In the healthcare industry, AI-powered image classification and segmentation have proven to be incredibly beneficial. Medical professionals can now use AI algorithms to accurately identify and classify different types of diseases or abnormalities in medical images such as X-rays, MRIs, or CT scans. This not only helps in faster diagnosis but also reduces the chances of human error.

Additionally, AI algorithms can segment specific areas of interest within an image, allowing doctors to focus on particular regions for closer examination or treatment planning.

Another industry greatly benefiting from AI is agriculture. With the help of image classification and segmentation techniques, farmers can monitor crop health more efficiently and effectively. By analyzing aerial images captured by drones or satellites, AI algorithms can identify areas where crops may be stressed due to pests, diseases, or nutrient deficiencies. This enables farmers to take timely action such as targeted pesticide application or providing additional nutrients to improve crop yield and quality.

Moreover, image segmentation allows for precise mapping of fields and accurate counting of plants, which aids in optimizing irrigation systems and reducing water wastage.

The retail industry is also reaping the rewards of AI-based image classification and segmentation technologies. With these advancements, retailers can enhance customer experiences by providing personalized recommendations based on their visual preferences. For example, a clothing retailer can use AI algorithms to analyze customer photos or browse history in order to suggest outfits that match their style preferences or latest fashion trends.

Furthermore, image segmentation techniques allow retailers to automatically extract product attributes like color or pattern from images uploaded by customers on social media platforms. This valuable data can then be used for market research purposes or for improving inventory management.

The applications of AI in various industries are vast and diverse thanks to advancements in image classification and segmentation technologies. From healthcare to agriculture and retail sectors - all are benefitting from the ability of AI algorithms to analyze visual data and make informed decisions. By harnessing the power of AI, these industries are enhancing their capabilities, optimizing processes, and ultimately improving customer experiences.

Now let's explore how AI is further enhancing daily experiences with smart visual recognition technology.

Enhancing Daily Experiences with Smart Visual Recognition

Enhancing our daily experiences, smart visual recognition technology uses advanced algorithms to analyze and interpret visual data, revolutionizing the way we interact with our surroundings. This technology has found applications in various fields, from healthcare to retail and entertainment. By leveraging artificial intelligence (AI), image classification and segmentation systems can accurately identify objects, people, and scenes in real-time.

Improving safety: One of the key benefits of smart visual recognition is enhancing safety in different environments. For example, in transportation, AI-powered cameras can detect road signs, traffic lights, and pedestrians to alert drivers about potential hazards. Similarly, surveillance systems equipped with this technology can quickly identify suspicious activities or intruders in public spaces or private properties.

Personalized shopping experiences: Smart visual recognition enables retailers to offer personalized shopping experiences to their customers. By analyzing facial expressions and body language, AI-powered systems can gauge customer preferences and emotions while they browse through products. This information allows retailers to provide tailored recommendations or even adjust store layouts based on customer behavior patterns.

Assisting medical professionals: In the healthcare industry, smart visual recognition plays a crucial role in assisting medical professionals during diagnosis and treatment processes. AI algorithms can analyze medical images such as X-rays or MRIs to detect abnormalities or assist with tumor segmentation for radiation therapy planning. This improves accuracy and efficiency while reducing human error.

Augmented reality gaming: Smart visual recognition also enhances gaming experiences by enabling augmented reality (AR) applications. Using a smartphone camera or dedicated AR devices like headsets, AI algorithms recognize real-world objects or markers and overlay digital content onto them in real-time. This creates immersive gaming experiences that blur the lines between virtual and physical worlds.

Through its ability to analyze visual data with precision and speed, smart visual recognition brings numerous benefits across various industries. From improving safety measures to offering personalized services, this technology continues to shape our daily lives by interacting with and interpreting the world around us.

Frequently Asked Questions

How does artificial intelligence actually classify and segment images?
Artificial intelligence uses complex algorithms to analyze images pixel by pixel. It identifies patterns and features to classify objects or segment different parts of an image. It's like a superpower that can instantly understand and organize visual information!

What are the limitations of image classification and segmentation using AI?
The limitations of image classification and segmentation using AI include difficulty in handling complex images, lack of robustness against variations in lighting or background, and potential biases in the training data.

Can AI algorithms differentiate between similar objects or images?

Yes, AI algorithms can differentiate between similar objects or images. They use advanced techniques like deep learning to analyze patterns and features, allowing them to distinguish even subtle differences with high accuracy.

Are there any ethical concerns related to the use of AI in image classification and segmentation?
Yes, there are several ethical concerns related to the use of AI in image classification and segmentation. These include issues of privacy, bias, discrimination, and potential misuse of personal data.

How can AI-powered image recognition systems be improved in terms of accuracy and efficiency?
To improve the accuracy and efficiency of AI-powered image recognition systems, you can enhance the training data quality, use advanced machine learning algorithms, optimize hardware infrastructure, and regularly update the models with new data.

Conclusion

In conclusion, you've learned about the fascinating world of AI and its applications in image classification and segmentation. Through this section, we've explored how AI has revolutionized various industries by providing accurate and efficient visual recognition capabilities.

From healthcare to retail, AI is enhancing daily experiences by analyzing images with precision and speed. Imagine walking into a store where AI-powered systems instantly recognize your preferences based on past purchases, offering personalized recommendations that make your shopping experience effortless.

Picture a medical professional using AI algorithms to accurately diagnose diseases from medical images, saving lives through early detection. These are just a few examples of how AI is transforming our world.

As technology continues to evolve, the possibilities for image classification and segmentation are endless. From self-driving cars to augmented reality applications, the future holds exciting advancements that will further enhance our lives.

So next time you snap a photo or search for an image online, remember that behind the scenes, there's an intelligent system at work, analyzing and categorizing visual data to provide us with valuable insights. Embrace this new era of smart visual recognition powered by AI – it's here to stay!

Applications of Computer Vision in Various Industries

Imagine a doctor using AI and computer vision to diagnose diseases more accurately and efficiently. With the help of advanced algorithms, these technologies can analyze medical images such as X-rays or MRIs, spotting even the tiniest abnormalities that might go unnoticed by human eyes. This revolutionary approach is transforming healthcare diagnostics, leading to faster diagnoses and ultimately saving lives.

But it doesn't stop there! Industries like manufacturing are also benefiting from computer vision. Imagine a factory where machines equipped with cameras continuously monitor production lines in real-time. By analyzing every product for defects or inconsistencies with incredible speed and accuracy, computer vision systems ensure that only high-quality items reach customers' hands. It's like having an extra set of eyes that never get tired or distracted!

Key Takeaways

- AI and computer vision are revolutionizing healthcare diagnostics by analyzing medical images with precision and speed.
- Computer vision enhances quality control processes in manufacturing by automating inspections and identifying defects or anomalies in products.
- Autonomous driving utilizes computer vision to improve road safety and efficiency through accurate object detection and adaptive cruise control.
- Computer vision technology in retail analyzes customer behavior and preferences in real-time, optimizing inventory and providing personalized experiences.

Healthcare: Revolutionizing Diagnostics with Computer Vision

Computer vision is revolutionizing diagnostics in healthcare, allowing doctors to accurately detect and diagnose diseases using AI-powered technology. With computer vision, medical professionals can analyze medical images such as X-rays, MRIs, and CT scans with incredible precision.

This technology can quickly identify abnormalities, assisting doctors in making accurate diagnoses and providing timely treatments for patients. By harnessing the power of artificial intelligence and computer vision algorithms, healthcare providers are able to improve patient outcomes significantly.

Computer vision can assist in early detection of diseases like cancer by identifying subtle signs that may be missed by human eyes alone. Moreover, it enables doctors to monitor disease progression over time by comparing images taken at different intervals. This data-driven approach enhances the accuracy of diagnoses and allows for personalized treatment plans tailored to each patient's specific needs.

Nowadays, computer vision systems can even surpass human capabilities in some areas. With advanced algorithms, these systems can analyze large quantities of data much faster than a human expert could ever accomplish. As a result, doctors have more time to focus on patient care rather than spending valuable hours manually reviewing medical images.

By seamlessly integrating computer vision into their workflow, healthcare professionals can streamline their processes and provide more efficient and accurate diagnoses.

With the revolution brought about by computer vision in healthcare diagnostics complete, let's dive into another exciting application: manufacturing! In this industry too, computer vision is enhancing quality control processes by automating inspections and ensuring products meet high standards consistently.

Manufacturing: Enhancing Quality Control with Computer Vision

Imagine how much more confident you'd feel about the quality of products if you could enhance your manufacturing processes with the power of advanced visual technology. Well, computer vision is making this a reality in the manufacturing industry.

By incorporating artificial intelligence and computer vision systems into their operations, manufacturers can significantly improve their quality control processes. These systems are capable of inspecting products at high speeds and identifying any defects or anomalies that may occur during production. This level of accuracy ensures that only products meeting the highest standards are released to the market.

With computer vision, manufacturers can automate various aspects of their quality control procedures. Instead of relying solely on human inspectors, who may be prone to fatigue or errors, computer vision systems can tirelessly monitor every product that passes through the assembly line. They use sophisticated algorithms to analyze images or videos captured by cameras installed strategically within the production process. Any deviations from established parameters are promptly detected and flagged for immediate attention. This not only saves time but also minimizes costly mistakes that might otherwise go unnoticed until later stages, resulting in improved overall efficiency.

Incorporating computer vision into manufacturing processes is revolutionizing quality control by enhancing precision and consistency like never before. By ensuring product defects are caught early on, manufacturers can reduce waste and save costs associated with rework or customer returns. Moreover, this advanced visual technology allows companies to continuously improve their production methods based on real-time data analysis from these systems' findings. Ultimately, harnessing the power of computer vision in manufacturing helps businesses deliver superior-quality products consistently while optimizing resources and streamlining operations.

By enhancing quality control with computer vision technology in manufacturing, companies gain a competitive edge in today's fast-paced market environment where customer expectations continue to rise rapidly.

However, this is just one example of how artificial intelligence is transforming industries across the board! Autonomous driving is another exciting application where computer vision plays a crucial role in improving safety and efficiency on our roads without human intervention required for certain tasks.

Autonomous Driving: Improving Safety and Efficiency through Computer Vision

By incorporating advanced visual technology, autonomous driving enhances road safety and efficiency by utilizing computer vision systems. These systems allow vehicles to perceive their surroundings and make informed decisions in real-time.

Here are three key ways in which computer vision improves autonomous driving:

- Object Detection: Computer vision enables autonomous vehicles to accurately detect and identify various objects on the road, such as pedestrians, cyclists, other vehicles, and traffic signs. By constantly monitoring the environment using cameras and sensors, these systems can anticipate potential hazards and respond accordingly. This capability greatly reduces the risk of accidents caused by human error or lack of attention.

- Lane Departure Warning: Another important application of computer vision in autonomous driving is lane departure warning. Using image recognition algorithms, the system can determine whether a vehicle is drifting out of its designated lane without signaling. If detected, it can alert the driver or even intervene by automatically steering the vehicle back into the correct lane. This feature helps prevent collisions due to unintentional lane changes.

- Adaptive Cruise Control: Computer vision plays a crucial role in adaptive cruise control (ACC), which maintains a safe distance from the vehicle ahead while traveling at a consistent speed. By analyzing images captured by cameras mounted on the car's front grille, ACC systems can detect other vehicles' positions and adjust speed accordingly. This not only ensures adequate

AI FUNDAMENTALS

spacing between vehicles but also optimizes fuel efficiency by avoiding unnecessary braking and acceleration.

With these advancements in computer vision technology for autonomous driving, roads become safer for everyone involved while improving overall traffic flow efficiency.

As we move forward into discussing how computer vision transforms retail experiences next...

Retail: Transforming the Customer Experience with Computer Vision

When you step into a retail store, the technology surrounding you seamlessly enhances your shopping experience through computer vision systems. These systems, equipped with cameras and sensors, are able to analyze customer behavior and preferences in real-time. For example, they can identify which products customers pick up and put back on the shelves, allowing retailers to understand popular items and optimize their inventory accordingly.

Additionally, computer vision can be used for facial recognition, enabling personalized experiences such as targeted advertisements or customized recommendations based on previous purchases. With this technology in place, shopping becomes more efficient and tailored to your individual needs.

Moreover, computer vision in retail goes beyond just improving efficiency; it also aims to provide a more interactive and immersive shopping experience. Augmented reality (AR) is one application that utilizes computer vision to overlay digital information onto the physical environment. Imagine trying on clothes virtually without actually putting them on or visualizing how furniture would look in your home before making a purchase. Computer vision enables these possibilities by accurately mapping virtual objects onto real-world scenes. This not only saves time but also allows you to make more informed decisions while exploring different options.

When you enter a retail store today, computer vision is at work behind the scenes to enhance your overall shopping experience. By analyzing customer behavior and preferences in real-time, it helps retailers optimize their inventory and provide personalized recommendations. Furthermore, through applications like augmented reality, computer vision transforms the way we interact with products by providing virtual try-on experiences and visualizing how items would fit into our lives.

With all these advancements in place, shopping has become more convenient and engaging than ever before – transitioning seamlessly into the next section about 'entertainment: enriching visual experiences with computer vision'.

Entertainment: Enriching Visual Experiences with Computer Vision

Step into a world where your favorite movies and TV shows come alive, thanks to the immersive visual experiences enabled by computer vision technology. With computer vision, entertainment industries are able to enhance their storytelling capabilities and create truly captivating experiences for audiences.

Whether it's through virtual reality, augmented reality, or advanced special effects, computer vision is revolutionizing the way we consume entertainment.

- Computer vision technology allows filmmakers to seamlessly blend real-world footage with CGI (computer-generated imagery), creating stunning visual effects that were once only possible in our wildest imaginations. From epic battle scenes in fantasy films to futuristic cityscapes in science fiction movies, computer vision brings these imaginative worlds to life with incredible detail and realism.

- Imagine watching a superhero movie where the hero's superpowers are enhanced through augmented reality overlays. With computer vision, filmmakers can seamlessly integrate these digital elements into the live-action footage, making it appear as though they are part of the physical world.

- Additionally, virtual reality experiences powered by computer vision allow viewers to step into their favorite movies and become active participants in the story. This level of immersion takes entertainment to a whole new level and creates unforgettable memories for audiences.

In addition to film and television, computer vision is also transforming other forms of entertainment such as gaming and live performances. In gaming, computer vision enables more realistic graphics and immersive gameplay experiences. Characters can react dynamically to players' movements and environments can adapt based on real-world data captured through cameras or sensors.

- For instance, imagine playing a horror game where the enemies' behavior is influenced by your own body language or facial expressions captured through your webcam. Computer vision makes this type of interactive gaming experience possible.

- Live performances are also being enhanced through computer vision technology. Concerts now incorporate projection mapping techniques that use cameras and sensors to precisely map visuals onto stages or performers in real-time. This creates visually stunning displays that synchronize perfectly with music or dance performances.

Step into a world where your favorite movies and TV shows come alive, thanks to the immersive visual experiences enabled by computer vision technology. With computer vision, entertainment industries are able to enhance their storytelling capabilities and create truly captivating experiences for audiences.

- Computer vision technology allows filmmakers to seamlessly blend real-world footage with CGI (computer-generated imagery), creating stunning visual effects that were once only possible in our wildest imaginations. From epic battle scenes in fantasy films to futuristic cityscapes in science fiction movies, computer vision brings these imaginative worlds to life with incredible detail and realism.

- Imagine watching a superhero movie where the hero's superpowers are enhanced through augmented reality overlays. With computer vision, filmmakers can seamlessly integrate these digital elements into the live-action footage, making it appear as though they are part of the physical world.

- Additionally, virtual reality experiences powered by computer vision allow viewers to step into their favorite movies and become active participants in the story. This level of immersion takes entertainment to a whole new level and creates unforgettable memories for audiences.

In addition to film and television, computer vision is also transforming other forms of entertainment such as gaming and live performances. In gaming, computer vision enables more realistic graphics and immersive gameplay experiences. Characters can react dynamically to players' movements and environments can adapt based on real-world data captured through cameras or sensors.

- For instance, imagine playing a horror game where the enemies' behavior is influenced by your own body language or facial expressions captured through your webcam. Computer vision makes this type of interactive gaming experience possible.

- Live performances are also being enhanced through computer vision technology. Concerts now incorporate projection mapping techniques that use cameras and sensors to precisely map visuals onto stages or performers in real-time. This creates visually stunning displays that synchronize perfectly with music or dance performances.

Frequently Asked Questions

How does computer vision technology help in diagnosing diseases in the healthcare industry?
Computer vision technology helps diagnose diseases in healthcare by analyzing medical images and identifying patterns or abnormalities. It can assist doctors in early detection, accurate diagnosis, and treatment planning, ultimately improving patient outcomes.

Can computer vision technology detect defects in products during the manufacturing process?
Yes, computer vision technology can detect defects in products during the manufacturing process. It uses advanced algorithms to analyze images and identify any abnormalities, helping ensure high-quality production and reducing errors.

How does computer vision contribute to enhancing safety in autonomous driving?
Computer vision enhances safety in autonomous driving by analyzing real-time data from cameras and sensors. One interesting statistic is that it can detect objects up to 200 meters away, helping vehicles make better decisions and prevent accidents.

In what ways can computer vision improve the customer experience in the retail industry?
Computer vision can enhance the customer experience in retail by analyzing shopper behavior, providing personalized recommendations, and enabling checkout-free shopping. It improves convenience, efficiency, and satisfaction for customers in stores or online.

How does computer vision enhance visual experiences in the entertainment industry?
Computer vision enhances visual experiences in the entertainment industry by enabling immersive virtual reality, augmented reality, and motion capture technologies. It allows for realistic graphics, interactive gaming, and seamless integration of digital elements into live performances.

Conclusion

So, there you have it, a glimpse into the incredible world of computer vision and its applications in various industries.

From healthcare to manufacturing, autonomous driving to retail, and even entertainment, this technology is revolutionizing the way we live and work.

Imagine a future where doctors can accurately diagnose diseases at an early stage, saving countless lives.

Picture a world where factories produce flawless products every single time, ensuring customer satisfaction.

Envision a society where cars navigate the roads seamlessly and accidents become a thing of the past.

And think about how computer vision can enhance your shopping experience or transport you to immersive virtual worlds.

The possibilities are truly endless with computer vision. It has the power to transform our lives in ways we never thought possible.

So, embrace this exciting technology and get ready for a future filled with innovation and extraordinary possibilities.

It's time to witness firsthand the magic that computer vision can bring to our world.

CHAPTER 8: ROBOTICS AND AUTOMATION

Robotics involves the design, creation, and operation of robots – machines that can perform tasks autonomously or with minimal human intervention.

On the other hand, automation refers to the use of technology to control and operate processes without human involvement.

Together, robotics and automation are revolutionizing various industries and impacting our daily lives in ways we may not even realize.

Imagine a future where robots assist us in our day-to-day activities, making them easier and more efficient.

From self-driving cars that navigate through traffic seamlessly to robotic vacuum cleaners that keep our homes clean without any effort on our part – these are just a few examples of how robotics is already transforming everyday life.

Automation takes it a step further by streamlining processes in industries like manufacturing, healthcare, agriculture, and logistics.

It eliminates repetitive tasks and frees up human workers to focus on more complex and creative endeavors.

Key Takeaways

- Robotics and automation revolutionize industries and impact daily lives.
- Robots assist in day-to-day activities, making them easier and more efficient.
- Automation streamlines processes in manufacturing, healthcare, agriculture, and logistics.
- Robots perform tasks autonomously or with minimal human intervention.

The Basics of Robotics and Automation

Now, let's dive into the basics of robotics and automation so you can understand how these incredible technologies work.

Robotics is all about creating machines that can perform tasks autonomously or with minimal human intervention. These machines, called robots, are designed to mimic human actions and movements. They're equipped with sensors to perceive their environment and actuators to interact with it.

Automation, on the other hand, refers to using technology to make processes more efficient by reducing the need for human involvement.

In simple terms, robots are like super-powered tools that can be programmed to perform specific tasks. They come in all shapes and sizes - from large industrial robots used in factories to small robotic vacuum cleaners in our homes. These machines are capable of carrying out repetitive or dangerous tasks that humans may find tedious or risky. For example, robots can assemble products on an assembly line much faster and with greater precision than humans ever could.

Automation plays a crucial role in various industries and everyday life. It involves using technology such as computers, software programs, sensors, and control systems to streamline processes and increase productivity. In manufacturing, automation allows for mass production at a faster rate while maintaining consistent quality standards. In transportation, automated systems help manage traffic flow and improve safety on roads. Even in our homes, automation has become increasingly common with smart devices like thermostats that adjust temperature settings based on our preferences.

Understanding the basics of robotics and automation gives us a glimpse into the immense potential these technologies hold for transforming various aspects of our lives. From improving efficiency in industries to simplifying daily tasks at home, robotics and automation continue to revolutionize the way we live and work without taking any major steps forward from here onwards. With ongoing advancements and integration of artificial intelligence, machine learning, and the Internet of Things (IoT), the possibilities for robotics and automation are boundless, promising to reshape entire industries, enhance productivity, and create new opportunities for innovation and growth.

Applications of Robotics in Everyday Life

Furthermore, the integration of robots into various aspects of our daily lives has led to an array of practical applications that enhance efficiency and convenience. Robots are now commonly used in industries such as manufacturing, healthcare, agriculture, transportation, and even in our homes.

Here are some examples of how robotics is making a difference in everyday life:

- In manufacturing, robots have revolutionized production lines by automating repetitive tasks. They can assemble products with great precision and speed, leading to increased productivity and cost savings for companies. This automation has also improved worker safety by taking over hazardous or physically demanding jobs.

- In healthcare, robots are being used for various purposes such as surgery assistance, patient monitoring, and medication dispensing. Surgical robots can perform minimally invasive procedures with greater accuracy than human surgeons. Additionally, robotic exoskeletons are helping patients with mobility issues regain their independence and improve their quality of life.

- In agriculture, robots are transforming farming practices. They can autonomously plant seeds, monitor crop health using sensors and drones, and even harvest crops efficiently. These advancements not only increase agricultural productivity but also reduce the need for manual labor and minimize environmental impact.

- In transportation, self-driving cars are becoming increasingly common on our roads. These vehicles use a combination of sensors and artificial intelligence to navigate without human intervention. The potential benefits include reduced traffic congestion, improved road safety through decreased human error accidents, and increased accessibility for people who cannot drive themselves.

- Finally, in our homes, we have seen the rise of smart devices such as robotic vacuum cleaners and personal assistants like Amazon's Alexa or Google Home. These robots make our lives more convenient by performing tasks like cleaning or playing music upon voice command.

With these practical applications already in place across various sectors of society comes a range of advantages that automation brings to different industries.

Advantages of Automation in Various Industries

Embrace the future and discover how automation is revolutionizing industries, providing countless benefits and advancements in efficiency and productivity.

One of the major advantages of automation in various industries is increased speed and accuracy. By replacing manual labor with automated systems, tasks can be completed at a much faster rate, reducing production time and increasing output. Automation also eliminates the possibility of human error, ensuring that processes are carried out with precision and consistency.

Another advantage of automation is improved safety for workers. In industries such as manufacturing or construction where there may be hazardous conditions or heavy machinery involved, automation allows for dangerous tasks to be performed by robots or machines instead of humans. This reduces the risk of accidents and injuries, creating a safer working environment for employees.

Furthermore, automation leads to cost savings for businesses. While implementing automated systems may require an initial investment, it ultimately results in long-term cost reductions. Automated processes are more efficient and require less manpower, leading to lower labor costs. Additionally, automation minimizes waste by optimizing resource utilization and reducing errors, which can save money on materials and resources.

As we look towards the future of robotics and automation, it's clear that these technologies will continue to play a significant role in transforming industries across various sectors. From self-driving cars revolutionizing transportation to robotic surgeries improving healthcare outcomes, the potential applications are vast. Embracing these advancements will not only lead to increased efficiency but also open up new opportunities for innovation and growth in our ever-evolving world.

The Future of Robotics and Automation

Get ready to witness the incredible advancements that'll shape your world - robotics and automation are paving the way for a future filled with limitless possibilities. As technology continues to evolve at an unprecedented pace, here are some exciting developments you can expect in the near future:

- Enhanced productivity: With robots taking over repetitive tasks, humans can focus on more complex and creative work. This increased efficiency will lead to higher productivity levels across industries.

- Improved safety: Robots equipped with sensors and advanced algorithms can perform hazardous tasks without risking human lives. From exploring dangerous environments to handling toxic substances, automation will make workplaces safer than ever before.

- Personalized healthcare: Imagine having a robot companion that monitors your health, reminds you to take medication, and assists with daily activities. Robotics has the potential to revolutionize healthcare by providing personalized care and support for individuals of all ages.

- Smarter homes: Automation is making its way into our households, simplifying our lives through smart home devices. From voice-controlled assistants that manage household chores to self-driving vacuum cleaners, robots will transform our living spaces into intelligent ecosystems.

- Sustainable solutions: Robotics and automation offer innovative solutions for sustainable development. From autonomous vehicles reducing carbon emissions to drones planting trees, these technologies have the power to address environmental challenges effectively.

With these remarkable advancements in robotics and automation just around the corner, we're entering an era where machines will work alongside humans seamlessly. The impact of this collaboration on society goes beyond convenience; it'll reshape industries, redefine job roles, and create new opportunities for growth and innovation.

The Impact of Robotics and Automation on Society

Robots and automation are set to unleash a tidal wave of change, revolutionizing society and leaving no aspect untouched in their wake. The impact of these advancements on society is both profound and far-reaching.

One area that will see significant changes is the workforce. As robots become more capable and efficient, they will take over many repetitive and mundane tasks currently performed by humans. This may lead to job displacement for some, but it also presents new opportunities for skill development and innovation.

Another major impact of robotics and automation on society is improved efficiency and productivity. Robots can work tirelessly without fatigue or breaks, resulting in faster production processes and higher output levels. This increased efficiency has the potential to lower costs for businesses, which can then be passed on to consumers in the form of lower prices. Additionally, with robots handling dangerous or physically demanding tasks, there may be a decrease in workplace accidents and injuries.

The integration of robotics and automation into various industries will also bring about changes in our daily lives. For instance, self-driving cars are becoming a reality, promising safer roads with reduced human error. Smart homes equipped with automated systems can optimize energy usage, making our lives more sustainable while providing convenience at the same time. Furthermore, advancements in healthcare robotics have the potential to improve patient care by assisting doctors during surgeries or providing companionship for the elderly.

The impact of robotics and automation on society cannot be overstated. From transforming the workforce to improving efficiency across industries to enhancing our daily lives, these advancements hold great promise for a better future. However, it's crucial that we navigate this technological revolution responsibly by ensuring proper training and support for those affected by job displacement while considering ethical implications such as privacy concerns or algorithmic biases. By doing so, we can harness the full potential of robotics and automation while minimizing any negative consequences along the way.

Frequently Asked Questions

How does the programming of robots work?

Programming robots involves writing instructions in a language that the robot understands. You tell the robot what to do step by step, using code. This allows the robot to perform tasks and complete actions autonomously.

Are there any risks or dangers associated with the use of robots and automation?
Yes, there are risks and dangers associated with the use of robots and automation. They can malfunction, causing physical harm or damage. Additionally, job displacement and privacy concerns are also potential risks to consider.

How do robots and automation impact job opportunities and employment?
Robots and automation are transforming job opportunities, potentially leaving some workers unemployed. But fear not, for this shift also presents new avenues for employment and the opportunity to adapt and thrive in a changing world.

What are the limitations or challenges faced by robotics and automation technology?
The limitations and challenges faced by robotics and automation technology include high costs, technical complexities, limited adaptability to new situations, ethical concerns, and the potential for job displacement.

How does artificial intelligence play a role in robotics and automation?
Artificial intelligence (AI) plays a crucial role in robotics and automation by enabling machines to learn, adapt, and make decisions. In fact, AI-powered robots are expected to create over 12 million jobs by 2025.

Conclusion

In conclusion, you now have a better understanding of the fascinating world of robotics and automation. You've learned about their basic principles and how they are applied in various aspects of everyday life.

From self-driving cars to robotic vacuum cleaners, these technologies have become an integral part of our society.

But the benefits don't stop there. Automation has revolutionized industries by increasing efficiency, reducing costs, and improving safety. It has made production processes faster and more precise, allowing companies to meet the demands of a rapidly changing market. With robots taking over repetitive tasks, human workers can focus on more complex and creative endeavors.

Looking ahead, the future holds even greater potential for robotics and automation. As technology advances, we can expect to see more sophisticated robots capable of performing intricate tasks with precision and agility. The integration of artificial intelligence will further enhance their capabilities, enabling them to learn from their surroundings and make autonomous decisions.

With each passing day, robotics and automation continue to shape our society in profound ways. They have transformed the way we live, work, and interact with one another. From transforming industries to enhancing our daily lives at home, these technologies have proven themselves indispensable.

So go forth with this newfound knowledge and embrace the robotic revolution! Who knows? Maybe one day you'll be living in a fully automated utopia where your every need is catered to by intelligent machines – okay, maybe not that extreme – but you get the idea!

Role of AI in Robotics and Automation

Are you curious about how Artificial Intelligence (AI) is revolutionizing the world of robotics and automation?

In this section, we will explore the role of AI in these fields and explain it to you in simple terms. AI refers to the ability of machines or computer systems to perform tasks that typically require human intelligence. It involves developing algorithms and models that enable machines to learn from data, make decisions, and carry out complex tasks with minimal human intervention.

Now, imagine combining the power of AI with robots - machines designed to interact with their physical environment. This intersection between AI and robotics has opened up a whole new realm of possibilities. By integrating AI into robots, they can become smarter, more adaptable, and capable of performing a wide range of tasks efficiently.

Whether it's navigating through unknown terrain, assembling intricate components in manufacturing processes, or even assisting in healthcare settings – robots powered by AI can handle these tasks effectively without constant human guidance.

The synergy between AI and robotics has led to significant advancements in automation across various industries, bringing us closer to a future where intelligent machines work alongside humans seamlessly.

Key Takeaways
- AI and robotics work together to create machines that can think and adapt like humans.
- AI-powered robots can perform complex tasks like navigating unknown terrain or assisting in healthcare.
- The integration of AI into robots has revolutionized industries such as manufacturing, healthcare, logistics, and agriculture.
- AI-powered automation enhances efficiency, productivity, decision making, safety, and resource management.

Understanding Artificial Intelligence (AI)

Artificial Intelligence, or AI, is mind-blowingly fascinating and has the power to revolutionize our world. It refers to the development of computer systems that can perform tasks that typically require human intelligence. These systems are designed to analyze data, make decisions, and solve problems just like a human would.

AI can be found in various forms such as virtual assistants like Siri or Alexa, recommendation algorithms used by streaming services, and even self-driving cars.

One of the key components of AI is machine learning. This involves training computers to learn from data patterns and improve their performance over time without being explicitly programmed for every task. Machine learning algorithms enable computers to detect patterns in large datasets and make predictions based on those patterns.

For example, an AI system can be trained with thousands of images of cats so that it learns how to identify a cat when it sees one in a new image.

The intersection of AI and robotics takes this technology a step further by incorporating it into physical machines. Robots equipped with AI have the ability to perceive their environment using sensors and cameras, process information using complex algorithms, and carry out actions based on their analysis. This allows them to perform tasks autonomously without constant human intervention.

The integration of AI into robots has opened up possibilities for automation in industries such as manufacturing, healthcare, agriculture, and logistics. With advancements in both fields happening at an unprecedented pace, we are witnessing rapid progress towards a future where robots will play increasingly significant roles in various aspects of our lives.

The Intersection of AI and Robotics

Imagine a world where machines can think and move like humans, seamlessly blending into our daily lives and performing tasks with the precision of a surgeon. This is the exciting intersection of artificial intelligence (AI) and robotics.

AI brings the ability to process massive amounts of data, learn from it, and make decisions based on that learning. When combined with robotics, AI enables machines to not only perform repetitive tasks but also adapt to new situations in real-time. It's like having an army of intelligent assistants at your disposal.

Robots equipped with AI can navigate complex environments, recognize objects, and interact with humans in natural ways. They can analyze their surroundings using cameras and sensors, allowing them to understand their environment and respond accordingly. For example, imagine a robot helping you cook dinner by fetching ingredients from the pantry or chopping vegetables precisely according to your instructions. With AI, robots have the potential to become valuable companions in our homes and workplaces.

By enhancing automation with AI, we are opening doors to unprecedented levels of efficiency and productivity. Imagine factories where robots work alongside humans seamlessly, taking care of repetitive or dangerous tasks while humans focus on more creative endeavors. With AI-powered automation, processes can be optimized for maximum output while minimizing errors. The integration of AI into robotics is revolutionizing industries such as manufacturing, healthcare, logistics, agriculture – virtually any field that involves repetitive or labor-intensive tasks.

The combination of AI and robotics holds immense potential for transforming our lives by creating intelligent machines that can perform a wide range of tasks autonomously. From assisting us in everyday activities to revolutionizing entire industries through enhanced automation processes - the possibilities are endless.

In the next section about 'enhancing automation with AI,' we will explore how this technology is being applied across various sectors for increased efficiency and improved outcomes without human intervention.

Enhancing Automation with AI

With the integration of AI, machines are becoming more efficient and productive, transforming industries across various sectors. Here are some exciting ways in which AI is enhancing automation:

- **Improved Decision Making:** AI-powered algorithms enable machines to analyze large amounts of data and make informed decisions in real-time. This allows automation systems to optimize processes, identify patterns, and adjust their actions accordingly.

- **Enhanced Safety:** By combining AI with robotics, we can create safer working environments. AI algorithms can detect potential hazards and take preventive measures to avoid accidents. For example, in manufacturing plants, robots equipped with AI can navigate around obstacles or shut down automatically if they sense a human presence nearby.

- **Increased Precision:** With the help of AI, automation systems can perform tasks with unparalleled precision. Robots can be trained using machine learning techniques to carry out intricate operations such as surgical procedures or assembling delicate components. This level of accuracy results in higher quality outputs and reduces errors.

- **Efficient Resource Management:** AI enables machines to optimize resource allocation by analyzing data on usage patterns and demand fluctuations. This helps businesses streamline their operations by reducing waste and maximizing efficiency in areas like energy consumption, inventory management, and supply chain optimization.

- **Personalized Experiences:** In customer-centric industries like retail and hospitality, AI enhances automation by personalizing experiences for individuals. Chatbots powered by natural language processing (NLP) algorithms provide personalized recommendations or assistance based on individual preferences or previous interactions.

As you can see from these examples, the integration of AI into automation systems brings numerous benefits across different industries such as manufacturing, healthcare, logistics, and customer service. The capabilities of these intelligent machines are continuously expanding as technology advances further.

Now let's explore how this transformative technology finds applications in different industries without skipping a beat!

Applications of AI in Different Industries

From revolutionizing healthcare to transforming customer service, AI has become the secret ingredient that adds a touch of magic to industries across the board.

In healthcare, AI is being used to analyze vast amounts of medical data and assist in diagnosing diseases more accurately and efficiently. It can also help in predicting patient outcomes and suggesting personalized treatment plans. Additionally, AI-powered robots are being developed to perform surgeries with great precision, reducing the risk of human error. With these advancements, the healthcare industry is witnessing improved patient care and better overall outcomes.

In the customer service sector, AI chatbots are becoming increasingly popular. These virtual assistants have the ability to understand natural language and provide instant responses to customer queries, making it easier for businesses to handle large volumes of customer interactions. Moreover, AI algorithms can analyze customer behavior patterns and preferences, enabling companies to offer personalized recommendations and targeted marketing campaigns. This not only enhances customer satisfaction but also helps businesses boost their sales and improve their bottom line.

AI is not limited to just healthcare or customer service; it has found applications in various other industries as well.

For example, in manufacturing, AI-powered robots are being used for tasks such as assembly line automation and quality control inspections.

In finance, AI algorithms are employed for fraud detection and risk assessment purposes.

In transportation, self-driving cars powered by AI technology are being tested on public roads with the aim of improving road safety.

As we delve into advancements in AI and future possibilities without skipping a beat from here on out...

Advancements in AI and Future Possibilities

You might already be aware of the incredible advancements in AI, but did you know that the future possibilities are just as mind-boggling? The field of artificial intelligence is constantly evolving and pushing boundaries, opening up a world of exciting prospects.

Here are three future possibilities that will leave you amazed:

- Enhanced Human-Robot Collaboration: In the near future, we can expect robots to work alongside humans in a more seamless and collaborative manner. With advancements in AI, robots will become smarter and more capable of understanding human intentions and emotions. This means that they can assist us with complex tasks, adapt to our needs, and even provide emotional support when required. Imagine having a robot coworker who understands your strengths, weaknesses, and preferences, making your work life easier and more efficient.

- Autonomous Vehicles: Self-driving cars have already made significant strides in recent years thanks to AI technologies like computer vision and machine learning. However, the future holds even greater potential for autonomous vehicles. Imagine a world where all cars on the road are self-driving - this could lead to safer roads with fewer accidents caused by human error. Additionally, autonomous vehicles could optimize traffic flow by communicating with each other and coordinating their movements seamlessly.

- Personalized Healthcare: AI has immense potential to revolutionize healthcare by providing personalized treatment options for individuals based on their unique genetic makeup or medical history. With AI-powered diagnostic tools, doctors can make faster and more accurate diagnoses while predicting potential health issues before they arise. Furthermore, robotic assistants equipped with advanced AI algorithms can aid doctors during surgeries or provide care for patients in remote areas where access to healthcare is limited.

The future possibilities of AI are truly awe-inspiring! From enhanced collaboration between humans and robots to self-driving cars transforming transportation systems, and personalized healthcare improving medical outcomes – there's no doubt that we're heading towards an exciting era powered by artificial intelligence. Buckle up because the journey ahead promises endless innovation and discovery.

Frequently Asked Questions

How does AI technology impact job opportunities in the robotics and automation industry?

AI technology in robotics and automation expands job opportunities. It enables machines to perform complex tasks, freeing up humans for more creative and strategic roles. With AI, industries can increase efficiency, productivity, and innovation while creating new jobs in the process.

Can AI-powered robots replace human workers completely in certain industries?

AI-powered robots have the potential to replace human workers in certain industries. In fact, a study found that by 2030, up to 800 million jobs could be automated globally.

What are the ethical implications of using AI in robotics and automation?
The ethical implications of using AI in robotics and automation are significant. It raises concerns about job displacement, privacy invasion, bias in decision-making, and the potential for AI to be used for harmful purposes.

How does AI technology improve the efficiency and accuracy of automated systems?
AI technology improves the efficiency and accuracy of automated systems by continuously learning and adapting to new data. It can analyze large amounts of information quickly, make decisions based on patterns, and perform tasks with precision, reducing errors and increasing productivity.

Are there any potential risks or challenges associated with integrating AI into robotics and automation processes?
There are potential risks and challenges when integrating AI into robotics and automation processes. These include issues with data privacy, job displacement, and ethical concerns surrounding the decision-making abilities of AI systems.

Conclusion

So, there you have it, the role of AI in robotics and automation explained in layman's terms. We've explored how AI is the driving force behind the intelligence of robots, allowing them to perform tasks with human-like capabilities.

From self-driving cars to smart homes, AI has revolutionized the way we live and work.

But what does this mean for the future? Well, advancements in AI are happening at an exponential rate. Imagine a world where robots can not only perform tasks but also think critically and make decisions on their own. A world where automation is seamlessly integrated into every aspect of our lives, making things faster, easier, and more efficient.

The possibilities are endless. So, brace yourself for what's to come because AI is here to stay and it's only going to get better from here.

Get ready for a future where machines not only assist us but also become our partners in innovation. Exciting times lie ahead, so buckle up and prepare for a journey into a world powered by AI!

Applications of AI in Industrial Automation, Drones, and Self-Driving Cars

When it comes to industrial automation, AI plays a crucial role in streamlining processes. Imagine a factory where machines work seamlessly together without human intervention. With AI algorithms analyzing data and making intelligent decisions in real-time, tasks such as quality control and predictive maintenance become more efficient. Through machine learning techniques, systems can adapt and improve their performance over time based on patterns and feedback collected from sensors and other sources. Ultimately, this leads to increased productivity and reduced downtime for companies operating in the manufacturing sector.

In the realm of drones, AI is enhancing efficiency like never before. Drones equipped with AI capabilities can autonomously navigate through complex environments while avoiding obstacles or adjusting their flight path accordingly. This allows them to perform tasks such as aerial surveillance or package delivery with precision and speed. The integration of computer vision systems enables drones to recognize objects or people on their own, ensuring safe operations even in crowded areas. With AI-powered drones becoming increasingly common, we can expect advancements in fields like agriculture (monitoring crops), disaster response (search and rescue missions), or even entertainment (capturing stunning aerial footage).

So, buckle up as we delve into the exciting world of AI applications!

Key Takeaways

- AI revolutionizes various industries, such as industrial automation, drones, and self-driving cars.
- AI-powered robots in manufacturing plants can identify defects in products and make real-time adjustments, improving efficiency and productivity.
- AI algorithms in supply chain management can predict demand patterns and optimize inventory levels, leading to more efficient operations.
- Drones equipped with AI capabilities can autonomously navigate through complex environments and perform tasks like aerial surveillance or package delivery, enhancing safety and efficiency.

Streamlining Processes in Industrial Automation

Let's dive into how AI is making our lives easier by streamlining processes in industrial automation. With the help of AI, machines and robots are becoming more intelligent and capable of performing complex tasks with precision.

For example, in manufacturing plants, AI-powered robots can quickly identify defects in products and make real-time adjustments to improve quality. This not only saves time but also reduces human error, resulting in higher efficiency and productivity.

AI is also revolutionizing supply chain management. By analyzing large amounts of data, AI algorithms can predict demand patterns, optimize inventory levels, and even automate the ordering process. This means that companies can avoid stockouts or excess inventory, leading to cost savings and improved customer satisfaction.

Moreover, AI-enabled systems can detect anomalies or potential issues in the supply chain before they occur, allowing for proactive problem-solving.

AI is transforming industrial automation by automating tasks that were once performed by humans and improving overall efficiency.

Now let's shift gears and explore how AI is enhancing efficiency with drones without compromising safety or reliability.

Enhancing Efficiency with AI in Drones

Boost your understanding of how AI is revolutionizing the use of unmanned aerial vehicles, allowing them to operate more efficiently and effectively. Drones equipped with AI technology are able to analyze vast amounts of data in real-time, making them invaluable tools for various industries.

For example, in agriculture, drones can use AI algorithms to monitor crop health and identify areas that require attention. This not only saves time but also allows farmers to take proactive measures to ensure optimal crop growth.

AI-powered drones are also being used in disaster management and search-and-rescue operations.

With their ability to quickly navigate through difficult terrains and gather crucial information from above, these drones play a vital role in locating survivors or assessing the extent of damage caused by natural disasters. By leveraging AI capabilities such as object recognition and autonomous decision-making, drones can assist emergency response teams in making faster and more informed decisions.

As we delve further into the fascinating world of AI applications, it's important to note that this is just one aspect of how artificial intelligence is transforming our everyday lives. Now that you understand how AI enhances efficiency in drones, let's explore its role in self-driving cars.

The Role of AI in Self-Driving Cars

Self-driving cars are revolutionizing the way we travel by utilizing artificial intelligence (AI) algorithms to navigate roads, make decisions, and ensure passenger safety. These vehicles are equipped with various sensors, cameras, and powerful processors that constantly gather data from their surroundings.

Using this data, AI systems analyze road conditions, detect obstacles, and calculate optimal routes. One of the key advantages of AI in self-driving cars is its ability to react faster than human drivers. The AI algorithms can process vast amounts of information in real-time and make split-second decisions based on that data.

This enables self-driving cars to respond quickly to unexpected situations such as sudden lane changes or pedestrians crossing the road. Additionally, AI allows these vehicles to communicate with each other through a network known as Vehicle-to-Vehicle (V2V) communication. This further enhances safety by enabling self-driving cars to share information about their speed, position, and intentions with nearby vehicles.

AI plays a crucial role in self-driving cars by taking over driving tasks and ensuring passenger safety. The advancements in technology have made it possible for these vehicles to navigate roads autonomously using sophisticated algorithms and sensor systems. With AI at the helm, self-driving cars offer a glimpse into a future where transportation is safer and more efficient than ever before.

Improving Safety in Industrial Environments

Imagine walking into an industrial environment where safety is significantly enhanced, thanks to the power of AI. The integration of artificial intelligence in industrial automation has revolutionized workplace safety, ensuring a secure and protected environment for workers.

With AI systems constantly monitoring and analyzing data, potential hazards can be identified in real-time, allowing for immediate action to prevent accidents. This technological advancement provides peace of mind, knowing that you're working in an environment where your well-being is a top priority.

- AI-powered sensors detect any abnormal behavior or malfunctioning equipment, immediately alerting operators and preventing potential accidents.
- Machine learning algorithms analyze historical data to identify patterns and predict maintenance needs, reducing the risk of unexpected breakdowns or failures.
- Automated robotic systems equipped with AI technology can handle dangerous tasks, eliminating the need for human intervention in hazardous environments.
- Intelligent video surveillance systems monitor the premises 24/7, detecting unauthorized access or suspicious activities.

- Virtual reality simulations provide realistic training scenarios for emergency situations, enabling employees to practice their response skills without any actual risks.

As AI continues to shape various industries, its impact on daily life becomes more evident. The advancements made in industrial automation through the use of AI not only improve workplace safety but also enhance productivity and efficiency. By reducing the occurrence of accidents and promoting a secure working environment, AI enables workers to focus on their tasks without constant worry about their well-being.

Transitioning from this improved safety aspect into how AI permeates other areas of our lives seamlessly showcases its broad influence on society as a whole.

Impact of AI on Daily Life

Experience the transformative impact of AI on your daily life, as it seamlessly integrates into various aspects, revolutionizing the way you work, communicate, and even relax.

AI has become an integral part of our lives through virtual personal assistants like Siri or Alexa. These smart assistants use AI algorithms to understand and respond to our voice commands, making tasks such as setting reminders, answering questions, or playing music effortless and convenient. They learn from our interactions and adapt to our preferences over time, providing a personalized experience tailored to our needs.

AI also plays a significant role in social media platforms and online shopping. Have you ever noticed how accurate recommendations on Netflix or Amazon are? That's because they're powered by AI algorithms that analyze your previous choices and browsing history to suggest movies or products you might like. This not only saves your time but also helps discover new things based on your interests.

Furthermore, AI is transforming healthcare by enabling more accurate diagnoses and personalized treatments. Medical professionals can now leverage machine learning algorithms to analyze vast amounts of patient data quickly and accurately identify patterns that may indicate certain diseases or conditions. This leads to earlier detection of illnesses and more effective treatment plans tailored specifically for each individual patient.

AI is changing the way we live our lives by seamlessly integrating into various aspects such as virtual personal assistants, social media platforms, online shopping, and healthcare systems. It simplifies tasks through voice commands, provides personalized recommendations based on our preferences, and enhances healthcare outcomes with more accurate diagnoses and personalized treatments. Embrace the transformative power of AI in your everyday life!

Frequently Asked Questions

How does AI in industrial automation streamline processes and improve productivity?

AI in industrial automation streamlines processes and improves productivity by taking over repetitive tasks, optimizing workflows, and reducing errors. This saves time and resources, allowing you to focus on more meaningful and impactful work.

Can AI in drones really enhance efficiency and make them more effective in various industries?

AI in drones can greatly enhance efficiency and effectiveness in various industries. By utilizing advanced algorithms, drones can autonomously navigate, collect data, and perform tasks with precision, reducing human error and saving time.

What specific role does AI play in self-driving cars and how does it contribute to their functionality?

AI in self-driving cars acts as the brain, making split-second decisions like a seasoned driver. It uses sensors to perceive the world, algorithms to analyze data, and machine learning to improve its skills over time.

How does AI improve safety in industrial environments and what are some examples of its applications?

AI improves safety in industrial environments by constantly monitoring and analyzing data to detect potential hazards or malfunctions. It can also automate repetitive tasks, reducing human error. Examples include predictive maintenance, real-time monitoring, and robotic assistance.

What are some everyday examples of how AI impacts daily life and what are the potential future implications?

AI impacts daily life in countless ways. From voice assistants and smart home devices that make your life easier, to personalized recommendations on streaming platforms, AI is everywhere. In the future, AI could revolutionize healthcare and transportation even more.

Conclusion

In conclusion, the applications of AI in industrial automation, drones, and self-driving cars are transforming the way we live and work. AI streamlines processes in industrial automation, allowing tasks that were once time-consuming and prone to errors to be completed with ease and precision. This not only saves time but also enhances productivity and efficiency.

Furthermore, AI revolutionizes the world of drones by enabling them to perform tasks that were previously unimaginable. From aerial surveillance to package delivery, these intelligent machines are taking flight to new heights. And with the help of AI, self-driving cars are becoming a reality, promising safer roads and more convenient transportation for all.

But it doesn't stop there. The impact of AI extends beyond these industries into our daily lives. It has become an integral part of our smartphones, virtual assistants, and even home appliances. From voice recognition technology to smart home automation systems, AI makes our lives easier and more enjoyable.

So next time you see a drone soaring through the sky or hear about advancements in self-driving cars, remember that behind these marvels lies the power of artificial intelligence. It's a world where machines mimic human intelligence to simplify complex tasks and bring forth new possibilities. Embrace this technological era as we witness AI's transformative effects on society—it's truly a sight to behold!

Ethical Considerations and Challenges in AI-Driven Robotics

As advancements in artificial intelligence (AI) continue to shape our world, it is crucial to understand the potential impact on privacy and data security. You may be wondering how these intelligent robots can affect your personal information and whether they can keep it secure. We will explore this issue and discuss ways to ensure transparency and accountability in AI-driven robotics.

Another important aspect to consider when it comes to AI-driven robotics is addressing bias in AI algorithms. Have you ever wondered if these machines can make fair decisions without any prejudice? The reality is that biases can be inadvertently embedded within AI algorithms, leading to unfair outcomes or discrimination. We will examine this challenge and highlight efforts being made to mitigate bias in order to create more equitable systems.

Furthermore, the rise of AI-driven robotics has raised concerns about potential job displacement and its economic implications. You might be concerned about the effect of automation on employment opportunities or wonder how it could impact different industries. We will discuss these issues, exploring both the potential risks as well as opportunities presented by AI-driven robotics.

Lastly, ethical guidelines and regulations play a vital role in ensuring responsible development and deployment of AI-driven robotics. You may question whether there are any guidelines or regulations governing their use or if there should be stricter measures put in place. We will dive into these considerations, examining existing frameworks while also discussing the need for continued discussions around ethics as technology continues to advance.

In this article, we aim to provide you with a comprehensive understanding of the ethical considerations and challenges surrounding AI-driven robotics. By breaking down complex concepts into simpler terms, we hope to shed light on these important discussions happening at the intersection of technology, ethics, and society.

Key Takeaways

- Ethical guidelines and regulations are important in the development and deployment of AI-driven robotics.
- Transparency and accountability in the operations of AI-driven robotics are crucial.
- Bias in AI algorithms can lead to unfair outcomes and discrimination, so efforts should be made to mitigate it.
- Job displacement and economic implications of AI-driven robotics should be considered, and proactive measures like retraining programs and universal basic income policies should be implemented.

Impact on Privacy and Data Security

AI-driven robotics present numerous challenges when it comes to privacy and data security, as our personal information becomes vulnerable to exploitation by malicious actors. These robots are designed to collect and analyze vast amounts of data, including sensitive information such as biometric data, location tracking, and even personal conversations. This raises concerns about who has access to this data and how it is being used.

With the increasing integration of AI in our daily lives, it's crucial to address these issues and ensure that our privacy rights are protected. One major concern is the potential for unauthorized access or hacking of these robotic systems. As AI-driven robots become more advanced and connected to the internet, they can be targets for cybercriminals seeking valuable personal information. If a robot's security measures aren't up to par, hackers could gain access to sensitive data or even take control of the robot itself. This could have serious consequences, ranging from identity theft to physical harm if a malicious actor gains control over a robot's movements.

To mitigate these risks, it's essential for developers and manufacturers to prioritize strong encryption protocols and secure storage methods for personal data collected by AI-driven robots. Additionally, there should be strict regulations in place regarding how this data can be shared or sold. Transparency regarding what types of data are being collected and how they'll be used is also crucial in building trust between users and AI-driven robotics technologies.

Overall, ensuring privacy and data security in the realm of AI-driven robotics is an ongoing challenge that requires constant vigilance from both developers and users alike. By implementing robust security measures, promoting transparency, and holding companies accountable for their handling of personal data, we can navigate this complex landscape while protecting our privacy rights without compromising technological advancements.

Moving on from privacy concerns surrounding AI-driven robotics, another important aspect that needs attention is ensuring transparency and accountability in their operations.

Ensuring Transparency and Accountability

To truly grasp the impact of this technology, you must first understand the vital importance of transparency and accountability in ensuring its responsible use.

When it comes to AI-driven robotics, transparency refers to the ability to clearly understand how these systems make decisions and operate. It is crucial for developers and manufacturers to provide detailed information about the algorithms being used, as well as any biases or limitations that may be present. This allows users and stakeholders to have a better understanding of how these robots function and make informed decisions about their use.

Accountability goes hand in hand with transparency. It involves holding individuals or organizations responsible for the actions taken by AI-driven robots. In cases where these robots are involved in critical decision-making processes, such as healthcare or law enforcement, it is essential to establish mechanisms that ensure accountability. This can include having clear guidelines and regulations in place, conducting regular audits of system performance, and implementing mechanisms for redress if errors occur.

Transparency and accountability are fundamental pillars when it comes to the ethical use of AI-driven robotics. These principles enable us to understand how these systems work, identify potential biases or limitations, and hold individuals or organizations accountable for their actions. By ensuring transparency and accountability within this field, we can move towards a more responsible deployment of AI-driven robotics that benefits society as a whole.

Now let's explore how we can address bias in AI algorithms without compromising their functionality.

Addressing Bias in AI Algorithms

Let's now delve into how we can tackle bias in AI algorithms while maintaining their functionality.

Bias in AI algorithms occurs when the data used to train them is skewed or reflects societal prejudices. This can lead to unfair outcomes and perpetuate discrimination against certain groups of people. To address this issue, it is crucial to ensure that the datasets used for training are diverse and representative of different demographics. By incorporating a wide range of perspectives, we can minimize the risk of biased decision-making by AI systems.

One approach to addressing bias in AI algorithms is through regular audits and evaluations. These assessments should focus on identifying any biases present in the system's decision-making processes. By continuously monitoring the algorithm's outputs and comparing them with real-world outcomes, we can identify instances where bias may be influencing results. This allows us to make necessary adjustments and improvements to mitigate any potential harm caused by biased algorithms.

Moreover, promoting transparency in AI systems is essential for addressing bias. Users should have access to information about how these algorithms work and what criteria they use for decision-making. Additionally, organizations developing AI technologies must prioritize diversity within their teams, ensuring that individuals from various backgrounds contribute to the development process. By implementing these measures, we can work towards creating more fair and unbiased AI systems that benefit society as a whole.

Now let's transition into discussing potential job displacement and economic implications without forgetting ethics altogether. It is crucial to consider the potential job displacement and economic implications of AI systems while also prioritizing ethical considerations. While AI has the potential to automate tasks and increase efficiency, it may also lead to job losses in certain industries. Therefore, it is vital to proactively address these concerns by investing in reskilling and upskilling programs to ensure that individuals can adapt to the changing job market. Additionally, governments and organizations should explore policies such as universal basic income or job guarantees to provide stability and support for those affected by job displacement. By acknowledging the ethical dimensions of job displacement and economic implications, we can strive towards a future where AI benefits society while minimizing its negative consequences.

Potential Job Displacement and Economic Implications

Consider the potential ramifications of job displacement and economic shifts caused by AI systems, as you navigate the complex landscape of emerging technologies.

As AI-driven robotics continue to advance, there's a growing concern that automation may replace human workers in various industries. While this can lead to increased efficiency and productivity, it also raises questions about unemployment rates and income inequality.

As jobs become automated, individuals who were once employed in those roles may struggle to find new employment opportunities, leading to financial hardships for themselves and their families.

Furthermore, the economic implications of widespread job displacement cannot be ignored. With fewer people earning wages, consumer spending power may decrease, affecting businesses across different sectors. This could result in a ripple effect on the overall economy, potentially leading to recessions or economic downturns.

Additionally, there's a fear that AI systems could concentrate wealth in the hands of a few powerful corporations or individuals who own and control these technologies.

Considering these potential challenges surrounding job displacement and economic shifts caused by AI systems highlights the need for ethical guidelines and regulations. It's crucial for policymakers and industry leaders to develop frameworks that address not only bias in algorithms but also the impact on employment and income distribution.

By establishing proactive measures such as retraining programs for displaced workers or implementing universal basic income policies, we can strive towards creating an equitable future where technology benefits all members of society.

Ethical Guidelines and Regulations

As you navigate the complex landscape of emerging technologies, it's crucial to address the elephant in the room: the need for clear rules and regulations to ensure that AI systems are used responsibly and ethically.

With advancements in AI-driven robotics, there is a growing concern about potential risks and unintended consequences. Ethical guidelines and regulations play a vital role in mitigating these risks and ensuring that AI systems are developed, deployed, and used in a responsible manner.

One key aspect of ethical guidelines is transparency. It's important for developers and organizations to be transparent about how AI systems make decisions, what data they use, and how they handle privacy concerns. This transparency helps build trust among users and stakeholders while also allowing for accountability.

Additionally, guidelines should emphasize fairness by ensuring that AI systems don't discriminate against individuals based on factors such as race or gender. By addressing biases in algorithms and datasets, we can reduce the potential harm caused by unfair decision-making processes.

Another crucial element of ethical guidelines is human oversight. While AI systems can automate various tasks efficiently, it's essential to have humans involved in critical decision-making processes. Humans can provide context-specific knowledge, empathy, moral judgment, and ensure that decisions made by AI align with societal values. Guidelines should encourage collaboration between humans and AI systems rather than replacing one with the other completely.

Ethical guidelines and regulations are necessary to govern the development and deployment of AI-driven robotics responsibly. Transparency ensures accountability while fairness reduces discriminatory practices. Human oversight maintains moral judgment and aligns decisions with societal values.

As we continue to embrace the benefits of AI technology, it's imperative that we establish clear rules to ensure its ethical use for everyone's benefit.

Frequently Asked Questions

How can AI-driven robotics impact the privacy and data security of individuals?
AI-driven robotics can impact your privacy and data security by collecting and analyzing personal information without your consent. This can lead to the misuse or unauthorized access of your data, putting you at risk of identity theft or other privacy violations.

What measures are being taken to ensure transparency and accountability in the development and deployment of AI-driven robotics?
To ensure transparency and accountability in the development and deployment of AI-driven robotics, measures like clear documentation of algorithms, third-party audits, and public reporting are being implemented.

How are biases addressed in AI algorithms used in robotics, and what steps are being taken to minimize their impact?
To address biases in AI algorithms used in robotics, steps are being taken to minimize their impact. This includes creating diverse and inclusive datasets, conducting regular audits, and implementing guidelines for fair and unbiased decision-making processes.

What are the potential job displacement and economic implications associated with the increasing use of AI-driven robotics?
The increasing use of AI-driven robotics can potentially lead to job displacement and have economic implications. As robots take over certain tasks, workers may be displaced, causing unemployment

and a shift in the job market.

Are there any ethical guidelines and regulations in place to govern the use of AI-driven robotics, and if so, what are they?

Yes, there are ethical guidelines and regulations in place to govern the use of AI-driven robotics. These rules help ensure that robots are used responsibly and do not harm humans or violate their privacy.

Conclusion

In conclusion, as you've delved into the world of AI-driven robotics, you can see that there are numerous ethical considerations and challenges that need to be addressed. Privacy and data security issues arise due to the vast amount of personal information being collected by these technologies. It's crucial for companies and policymakers to prioritize ensuring transparency and accountability so that users can trust these robots without any doubt.

Moreover, bias in AI algorithms is a pressing concern. Artificial intelligence systems may unintentionally perpetuate discriminatory practices if they're trained on biased data sets. This could result in unfair treatment or decisions based on race, gender, or other sensitive factors. To avoid this, ongoing efforts must be made to address bias and develop unbiased algorithms.

As an example, scenario, imagine a healthcare robot assisting doctors in diagnosing patients' conditions. If the AI algorithm used by the robot has been trained predominantly on male patient data, it may struggle to accurately diagnose female patients due to inherent biases in the training data. This could lead to misdiagnoses or delayed treatments for women, highlighting the importance of addressing bias in AI algorithms.

Overall, as AI-driven robotics continue to advance swiftly into our lives, it's crucial for us all to actively consider and address the ethical implications they bring forth. By doing so, we can ensure that these technologies are developed responsibly and ethically while benefiting society as a whole.

CHAPTER 9: AI IN HEALTHCARE

Welcome to the world of healthcare, where cutting-edge technology meets compassionate care. Picture this: You're standing at the crossroads of innovation and healing, and you can't help but marvel at the wonders Artificial Intelligence (AI) has brought to this realm.

In this section, we'll delve into the importance of AI in healthcare, unraveling its impact on diagnosis, treatment, patient care, and ethical considerations.

Nowadays, AI isn't just a fancy term reserved for science fiction movies; it's become an invaluable tool that transforms how healthcare professionals work their magic. Just like a trusted sidekick guiding a superhero through perilous adventures, AI lends its remarkable capabilities to doctors and nurses across the globe.

By analyzing vast amounts of medical data faster than humanly possible, it helps identify patterns and trends that even the most astute medical minds might miss. With AI by their side, healthcare providers are empowered to make more accurate diagnoses and tailor personalized treatment plans for each patient's unique needs. It's like having a Sherlock Holmes-like companion who never misses a clue or an opportunity to save lives.

Understanding the Basics of Artificial Intelligence

Artificial Intelligence, or AI for short, is a field of computer science that focuses on creating intelligent machines capable of performing tasks that typically require human intelligence. These machines are designed to simulate human thinking processes such as learning, problem-solving, and decision-making.

In simpler terms, AI allows computers to think and act like humans, making them incredibly powerful tools in various industries.

One of the key components of AI is machine learning. This involves training computers to recognize patterns and make predictions based on large amounts of data. Just like how we learn from our experiences, machine learning algorithms enable computers to learn from vast datasets and improve their performance over time.

With this ability, AI systems can analyze complex medical data more accurately than ever before. They can quickly identify trends, detect anomalies, and even predict potential health risks or outcomes.

The applications of AI in healthcare are vast and far-reaching. By harnessing the power of AI, doctors and healthcare professionals can provide more accurate diagnoses, develop personalized treatment plans, and improve patient outcomes.

For example, AI algorithms can analyze medical images such as X-rays or MRIs with incredible precision to aid in early detection of diseases like cancer. Additionally, virtual assistants powered by AI can help patients manage their medications effectively by providing timely reminders or answering common health-related questions.

Now that you have an understanding of the basics of AI, let's explore its applications in healthcare without missing a beat!

Applications of AI in Healthcare

Explore the countless ways AI transforms the world of medicine, assisting doctors with diagnostics, analyzing patient data, and revolutionizing treatment plans. AI has become an indispensable tool in healthcare, offering a wide range of applications that benefit both patients and medical professionals. Here are some of the key areas where AI is making a significant impact:

- Medical imaging analysis: AI algorithms can analyze medical images such as X-rays, MRIs, and CT scans to detect abnormalities and assist in accurate diagnosis. This technology helps radiologists by highlighting potential areas of concern and improving their ability to identify diseases at an early stage.
- Predictive analytics: By analyzing large volumes of patient data, AI can predict disease outcomes and assess risks for individual patients. This information allows doctors to personalize treatment plans based on each patient's specific needs and increase the effectiveness of interventions.
- Virtual assistants: AI-powered virtual assistants like chatbots provide immediate access to reliable medical information and assistance 24/7. These digital tools can answer common health questions, offer symptom assessments, schedule appointments, and provide guidance for self-care.
- Drug discovery: Developing new drugs is a complex process that often takes years or even decades. AI algorithms can help researchers sift through vast amounts of data to identify potential drug candidates more efficiently. By accelerating this process, AI contributes to faster development and approval of life-saving medications.

With its ability to enhance medical imaging analysis, enable predictive analytics, provide virtual assistance, and facilitate drug discovery processes seamlessly behind the scenes, AI plays a pivotal role in improving diagnosis and treatment in healthcare settings.

Improving Diagnosis and Treatment with AI

Enhance your understanding of medical diagnosis and treatment through the transformative power of AI. With artificial intelligence, healthcare providers can rely on advanced algorithms to analyze vast amounts of patient data and provide accurate diagnoses.

AI systems can quickly sift through medical records, test results, and symptoms to identify patterns and potential conditions that may have been missed by human physicians. This not only saves time but also reduces the risk of misdiagnosis or delayed treatment.

Furthermore, AI has the potential to revolutionize treatment plans by tailoring them to individual patients. By analyzing a patient's genetic information, medical history, and lifestyle factors, AI algorithms can recommend personalized treatments that are more effective and have fewer side effects. This could lead to better outcomes for patients as they receive targeted therapies based on their unique characteristics.

Additionally, AI-powered tools can continuously monitor patients' vital signs during treatment, alerting healthcare professionals to any deviations from normal levels in real-time.

By improving diagnostic accuracy and personalizing treatment plans, AI has the potential to greatly enhance patient care and outcomes. With AI-enabled systems in place, healthcare providers can ensure that patients receive timely and appropriate interventions, resulting in better health outcomes overall.

Additionally, these technologies empower patients by providing them with valuable insights into their own health status and enabling them to make informed decisions about their care.

The integration of AI into healthcare holds great promise for transforming the way we diagnose and treat diseases while prioritizing patient well-being at every step.

Transition Sentence: As we delve further into how AI enhances patient care and outcomes in healthcare settings...

Enhancing Patient Care and Outcomes

Immerse yourself in the incredible impact of AI on patient care and outcomes as it revolutionizes the way medical professionals diagnose and treat diseases. AI technology has the potential to significantly enhance patient care by analyzing vast amounts of data and providing valuable insights that can lead to more accurate diagnoses and personalized treatment plans.

With AI, healthcare providers can access real-time information about a patient's condition, enabling them to make informed decisions quickly and effectively.

One way AI improves patient care is through predictive analytics. By analyzing a patient's health records, including medical history, lab results, and imaging scans, AI algorithms can identify patterns and predict potential health issues before they occur. This allows healthcare professionals to proactively intervene and prevent complications or provide early intervention for better outcomes. For example, AI-powered systems can detect subtle changes in vital signs or symptoms that may indicate a deteriorating condition, alerting caregivers to take immediate action.

Furthermore, AI-driven technologies empower patients by enabling remote monitoring and self-care management. Wearable devices equipped with sensors can continuously monitor vital signs such as heart rate, blood pressure, or glucose levels. These devices send real-time data to healthcare providers who can remotely track patients' progress and intervene if necessary. Patients themselves can also access their health data through mobile apps or online platforms, promoting self-awareness about their conditions and encouraging active participation in their own care.

As we explore the immense benefits of AI in enhancing patient care and outcomes, it is important to consider ethical considerations in this rapidly advancing field of healthcare technology. The use of personal health data raises concerns about privacy protection and security breaches. Additionally, there are questions surrounding the accountability of AI systems for diagnostic errors or treatment recommendations. These ethical challenges must be addressed through robust regulations that safeguard patient rights while harnessing the potential benefits of AI-driven healthcare innovation.

In conclusion, AI has revolutionized patient care by providing accurate diagnoses based on vast amounts of data analysis while also enabling remote monitoring and self-care management. However, as we embrace these advancements, it is crucial to carefully navigate the ethical considerations surrounding privacy protection and accountability. The next section will delve into the ethical implications of AI-driven healthcare and how they're being addressed to ensure the responsible use of this powerful technology.

Ethical Considerations in AI-Driven Healthcare

Step into the world of AI-driven healthcare and discover the ethical considerations that come with harnessing this groundbreaking technology. As AI continues to advance in healthcare, it's crucial to address the ethical implications that arise. Here are some key considerations:

- Privacy concerns: With AI analyzing vast amounts of patient data, there's a need to protect patient privacy and ensure data security. It's important to establish strict protocols for data collection, storage, and usage to prevent unauthorized access or breaches.
- Bias and discrimination: Algorithms used in AI systems are trained on large datasets, which may inadvertently perpetuate biases present in the data. This can lead to unequal treatment based on factors such as race or socioeconomic status. Efforts must be made to identify and mitigate these biases to ensure fair and equitable care for all patients.
- Transparency and explainability: AI algorithms often make decisions based on complex calculations that can be difficult for humans to understand. It's essential that healthcare providers have a clear understanding of how AI arrives at its conclusions so they can trust and verify its recommendations.
- Accountability: When using AI systems, there should be accountability for any errors or adverse outcomes. Establishing guidelines for who's responsible when something goes wrong is critical in ensuring patient safety and maintaining trust in the technology.

While AI has immense potential in revolutionizing healthcare, it also presents ethical challenges that must be addressed. By carefully considering privacy concerns, bias mitigation, transparency, and accountability, we can harness the power of AI while upholding ethical standards in delivering quality care to patients.

Frequently Asked Questions

How does artificial intelligence work in healthcare?

Artificial intelligence in healthcare works by analyzing large amounts of data, such as patient records and medical literature, to identify patterns and make predictions. It can assist in diagnosis, treatment planning, drug discovery, and even personalized medicine.

What are the potential risks associated with using AI in healthcare?

Potential risks associated with using AI in healthcare include inaccurate diagnoses, privacy breaches, and bias in algorithms. Are you willing to trust a machine with your health decisions?

Can AI replace doctors and healthcare professionals?

No, AI cannot replace doctors and healthcare professionals. While it can assist in diagnosis and treatment, human expertise is crucial for complex decision-making, empathy, and personalized care that machines cannot replicate.

How can AI technology improve patient monitoring and early detection of diseases?

AI technology can greatly enhance patient monitoring and early disease detection. Imagine a system that constantly analyzes your health data, alerting you and your doctor of any potential issues before they become serious.

What are the privacy concerns when it comes to using AI in healthcare?
Privacy concerns in using AI in healthcare include the potential for unauthorized access to sensitive medical data, breaches of patient confidentiality, and the risk of biased algorithms impacting treatment decisions. Protecting patient privacy is crucial for ethical and effective implementation of AI technology.

Conclusion

In conclusion, you now have a clearer understanding of the importance of AI in healthcare. By harnessing the power of artificial intelligence, medical professionals are able to enhance diagnosis and treatment methods, ultimately improving patient care and outcomes.

Like a skilled conductor leading an orchestra, AI orchestrates vast amounts of data to create harmonious melodies of knowledge that guide doctors towards more accurate diagnoses and effective treatments.

Furthermore, AI in healthcare is not just about technology - it's about humanity. It empowers doctors to make more informed decisions and provides patients with personalized care tailored to their specific needs. Just as a caring friend offers support during difficult times, AI supports healthcare providers by analyzing complex data and offering valuable insights that can save lives.

While AI brings tremendous benefits to the field of healthcare, we must also consider ethical considerations. As with any powerful tool, there is a need for responsible use and safeguards in place to protect patient privacy and ensure transparency in decision-making processes.

Overall, the integration of AI into healthcare is like adding wings to medicine's progress. It propels us forward into an era where precision medicine becomes the norm and personalized care reaches new heights.

So, embrace these technological advancements with open arms, for they hold immense potential to revolutionize how we approach healthcare delivery for the betterment of all.

Medical Image Analysis and Diagnostics

Are you curious about how artificial intelligence (AI) is revolutionizing the field of medical image analysis and diagnostics? In this section, we will explore the role of AI in this area.

With the rapid advancements in technology, AI has emerged as a powerful tool that can assist doctors and radiologists in interpreting medical images more accurately and efficiently.

Imagine this scenario: You have just undergone a medical imaging test such as an MRI or CT scan, and now your doctor needs to analyze the images to make a diagnosis. This is where AI comes into play. By utilizing complex algorithms, AI can analyze these images with incredible speed and precision, helping doctors identify abnormalities or potential diseases.

By assisting in early detection, AI can significantly improve patient outcomes by enabling timely interventions. Moreover, AI can also reduce the burden on radiologists by automating repetitive tasks like image segmentation or tumor detection. As a result, healthcare professionals can focus more on providing personalized care to patients rather than spending countless hours analyzing images manually.

In conclusion, AI has become an indispensable tool in medical image analysis and diagnostics due to its ability to enhance accuracy and efficiency while reducing workload for healthcare professionals.

Throughout this section, we will delve deeper into various aspects of AI in this field, including its advantages, challenges faced during implementation, future applications, as well as explaining complex algorithms in easy-to-understand terms.

Key Takeaways

- AI revolutionizes medical image analysis and diagnostics, making it faster and more accurate.
- AI helps doctors interpret medical images with speed and precision, improving patient outcomes.
- AI reduces the burden on radiologists by automating repetitive tasks and enhancing accuracy.
- AI can detect abnormalities or diseases in medical images, providing objective assessments and quantitative measurements.

The Role of AI in Medical Image Analysis

Artificial intelligence (AI) is revolutionizing medical image analysis by using advanced algorithms to assist doctors in interpreting and diagnosing various conditions. With its ability to process vast amounts of data quickly and accurately, AI has become an invaluable tool for healthcare professionals.

One of the primary roles of AI in medical image analysis is assisting in the detection of abnormalities or diseases. By analyzing medical images such as X-rays, CT scans, or MRIs, AI algorithms can identify patterns or anomalies that may not be easily discernible to the human eye. This helps doctors make more accurate diagnoses and develop appropriate treatment plans for their patients.

Additionally, AI can provide quantitative measurements and objective assessments of certain parameters within the images, further aiding clinicians in decision-making.

Another important aspect where AI excels is expediting the analysis process. Traditionally, radiologists would spend a significant amount of time reviewing and interpreting each image manually. However, with the assistance of AI algorithms, this time-consuming task can now be automated. By rapidly processing large volumes of medical images and flagging potential areas of concern for further review by doctors, AI helps streamline workflows and improves efficiency within healthcare systems.

You now have a glimpse into how AI assists with analyzing medical images. Its ability to detect abnormalities accurately while also expediting analysis processes has transformed diagnostic imaging practices. In the next section about "advantages of AI in diagnostic imaging," we will explore these benefits further without missing a beat!

Advantages of AI in Diagnostic Imaging

With AI's ability to interpret medical images, you can more accurately identify and treat conditions, like a guiding light in the darkness of diagnoses. AI algorithms can analyze large volumes of medical images in a fraction of the time it would take for a human doctor to do so. This means that potential abnormalities or patterns can be detected earlier, leading to faster diagnosis and treatment.

Additionally, AI systems can compare new images with vast databases of previous cases, helping doctors make more informed decisions based on similar cases from the past.

Another advantage of AI in diagnostic imaging is its ability to reduce errors and increase consistency. Human doctors may sometimes miss subtle signs or make errors when interpreting complex medical images. However, AI algorithms are trained using vast amounts of data and can detect even the most minute details that might go unnoticed by humans. By providing consistent results across different scans and reducing human error, AI helps improve the overall accuracy and reliability of diagnoses.

Furthermore, AI has the potential to improve patient outcomes by increasing efficiency in healthcare delivery. With faster analysis and interpretation of medical images, treatment plans can be initiated sooner, potentially saving lives or preventing further complications. Moreover, utilizing AI for diagnostic imaging allows doctors to focus more on patient care rather than spending excessive time analyzing images manually.

These advantages highlight how AI is revolutionizing medical image analysis, but implementing this technology comes with its own set of challenges in terms of ethics, privacy concerns, and regulatory frameworks that need to be addressed.

Transition: While there are many benefits to using AI in diagnostic imaging, there are also significant challenges that need to be overcome for successful implementation in healthcare settings without compromising patient safety or privacy...

Challenges in Implementing AI in Medical Diagnostics

Navigating the implementation of AI in medical diagnostics comes with a myriad of challenges that must be addressed to ensure the seamless integration of this groundbreaking technology. Here are three key challenges:

- **Data quality and availability:** AI algorithms rely on large amounts of high-quality data for training and validation. However, obtaining such datasets can be challenging in the field of medical diagnostics. Medical images are often complex and require meticulous annotations by experts, which can be time-consuming and resource-intensive. Additionally, there's a need to ensure that the data used for training AI models is diverse and representative of different patient populations to avoid biases in diagnosis.

- **Regulatory considerations:** Implementing AI in medical diagnostics raises important regulatory questions. Healthcare systems need to navigate through existing regulations surrounding patient privacy, data sharing, and liability issues when adopting AI technologies. It's crucial to establish transparent guidelines and protocols for integrating AI into clinical workflows while ensuring compliance with legal frameworks such as HIPAA (Health Insurance Portability and Accountability Act).

- **Clinical acceptance and trust:** Convincing healthcare professionals about the reliability and safety of AI-based diagnostic tools can be a significant challenge. There may be concerns regarding accuracy, accountability, or fear that these technologies might replace human expertise entirely. Building trust requires extensive validation studies, collaboration between researchers and clinicians, clear communication about limitations, as well as demonstrating tangible benefits like improved efficiency or reduced errors.

As we consider the challenges faced during implementation, it's important to recognize that addressing these obstacles will pave the way for future applications of AI in medical image analysis. By overcoming hurdles related to data quality, regulatory compliance, and clinical acceptance, we can unlock even more potential for using AI algorithms to improve diagnostic accuracy and patient outcomes in healthcare settings without compromising human expertise.

Future Applications of AI in Medical Image Analysis

Imagine a world where doctors can utilize advanced technology to analyze medical images with unprecedented accuracy, revolutionizing patient care and treatment options. This is the future that AI holds for medical image analysis. With the help of AI algorithms, medical professionals will be able to detect diseases and conditions at earlier stages, leading to more effective treatments and improved outcomes for patients.

AI can analyze large volumes of medical images in a fraction of the time it would take a human radiologist, allowing for faster diagnoses and reducing wait times. Not only can AI assist in diagnosing diseases, but it also has the potential to predict patient outcomes based on medical images. By analyzing patterns within the images, AI algorithms can identify subtle changes that may indicate disease progression or response to treatment. This information can guide doctors in making more informed decisions about patient care plans and interventions.

In addition to diagnostics and prediction, AI has the capability to assist in surgical planning and guidance. By integrating with surgical devices, AI algorithms can provide real-time feedback during procedures, helping surgeons navigate complex anatomical structures and ensure precise placement of instruments. This level of precision could minimize risks associated with surgeries while optimizing outcomes.

With these advancements on the horizon, it's crucial for both healthcare professionals and patients to understand how AI algorithms work in layman's terms. By demystifying the complexities behind this technology, individuals can become more educated consumers of healthcare services. Understanding how AI analyzes medical images allows patients to have meaningful conversations with their physicians about their diagnoses and treatment options.

So, let's delve into understanding AI algorithms in layman's terms and explore how they make sense of our medical images without requiring any technical expertise.

Understanding AI Algorithms in Layman's Terms

Exploring the incredible world of AI algorithms in a way that makes us feel excited and empowered to understand their impact on our healthcare is a fascinating journey.

Let's break it down into simpler terms. AI algorithms are like super smart computer programs that can analyze medical images, such as X-rays or MRIs, with incredible accuracy and speed. They use complex mathematical models and patterns to detect abnormalities or diagnose diseases.

Imagine you have an X-ray image of your lungs. The AI algorithm can scan through the image pixel by pixel, looking for any signs of abnormalities that may indicate a potential health issue like pneumonia or lung cancer. It can analyze thousands of images in seconds, comparing them to a vast database of known patterns and cases. This allows it to make accurate diagnoses based on similar cases it has learned from before.

The beauty of AI algorithms lies in their ability to continuously learn and improve over time. Each time they analyze an image; they gather more data and refine their understanding of different diseases. This means that as more medical images are analyzed using AI, its accuracy will only get better and better. It's like having an ever-growing library of medical knowledge at your fingertips, helping doctors make faster and more precise diagnoses for patients worldwide.

Frequently Asked Questions

What are the potential ethical concerns associated with using AI in medical image analysis and diagnostics?

Using AI in medical image analysis and diagnostics can raise serious ethical concerns. It could exaggerate minor issues, causing unnecessary stress for patients. Additionally, relying solely on AI may lead to misdiagnoses or neglecting the human aspect of healthcare.

How does AI technology improve the accuracy and efficiency of diagnostic imaging?

AI technology improves the accuracy and efficiency of diagnostic imaging by analyzing medical images quickly and accurately, allowing faster diagnoses. It can detect subtle details that may be missed by human eyes, leading to more precise treatment plans.

Are there any limitations or risks to relying solely on AI algorithms for medical image analysis?

Relying solely on AI algorithms for medical image analysis has limitations and risks. It may not yet be as accurate or reliable as human experts, and there is a potential for errors or misinterpretation of images.

Can AI algorithms be used to detect and diagnose all types of medical conditions?

Can AI algorithms really detect and diagnose all types of medical conditions? While they have shown promise in certain areas, there are limitations to their accuracy and reliability that need to be considered.

What steps are being taken to ensure the privacy and security of patient data in AI-based medical diagnostics?

To ensure privacy and security of patient data in AI-based medical diagnostics, steps include implementing strict access controls, encrypting data during transmission and storage, conducting regular audits, and adopting robust cybersecurity measures to prevent unauthorized access or breaches.

Conclusion

In conclusion, AI has revolutionized medical image analysis and diagnostics, providing numerous advantages and opportunities for the healthcare industry. With AI algorithms analyzing images with speed and precision, doctors can make accurate diagnoses and provide timely treatments to patients. This technology has the potential to greatly improve patient outcomes and save lives.

One interesting statistic that evokes emotion is that studies have shown that AI algorithms can detect certain diseases in medical images with a higher accuracy rate than human radiologists. For example, a study published in the journal Nature found that an AI algorithm correctly identified breast cancer in mammogram images 94.5% of the time, compared to an average accuracy rate of 88.2% for human radiologists. This statistic highlights the potential of AI to enhance diagnostic capabilities and ultimately improve patient care.

Imagine the impact this could have on early detection and treatment of diseases like cancer. With AI assisting radiologists, more cases can be accurately diagnosed at an early stage when treatment options are more effective. This statistic not only emphasizes the power of AI in healthcare but also instills hope for better health outcomes for individuals around the world.

In conclusion, while there are challenges in implementing AI in medical diagnostics, its potential benefits far outweigh any obstacles faced. The future applications of AI in medical image analysis hold immense promise for improving healthcare worldwide. By understanding these complex algorithms in layman's terms, we can appreciate how this technology is transforming medicine and positively impacting lives.

Predictive Modeling and Disease Prognosis

In this section, we will explore the role of AI in healthcare and how it is revolutionizing the field of disease prediction.

By analyzing patient data and using advanced algorithms, AI can accurately predict the progression of diseases, allowing for personalized treatment plans that lead to improved patient outcomes.

Imagine a future where doctors can accurately forecast how a disease will progress in an individual patient. With AI and predictive modeling, this future is becoming a reality.

By analyzing vast amounts of patient data, including medical records, genetic information, lifestyle factors, and even social determinants of health, AI algorithms can identify patterns and make accurate predictions about disease prognosis.

This means that doctors can develop personalized treatment plans tailored to each patient's specific needs, leading to better outcomes and more targeted interventions.

Key Takeaways

- AI and predictive modeling can analyze patient data to accurately predict disease progression and improve disease prognosis.
- Personalized treatment plans based on individual characteristics and risk factors can optimize successful outcomes in healthcare.
- AI algorithms can recommend treatment options and help doctors make informed decisions based on the specific characteristics of a patient's disease.
- The combination of predictive modeling and real-time monitoring enables proactive intervention and better management of chronic conditions.

The Role of Artificial Intelligence in Healthcare

With the help of AI, doctors are able to analyze large amounts of patient data, such as medical records, lab results, and imaging scans, to identify patterns and make predictions about a patient's future health outcomes.

This can be incredibly valuable in diagnosing diseases at an early stage and developing personalized treatment plans. By harnessing the power of AI, healthcare professionals can provide better care and improve patient outcomes.

One way AI is used in predictive modeling for disease prognosis is through machine learning algorithms.

These algorithms are trained on vast amounts of data from previous patients and learn to recognize patterns that indicate certain health conditions or predict the progression of a disease.

For example, an AI algorithm can analyze a patient's genetic information along with their medical history and lifestyle factors to determine their risk for developing certain diseases like cancer or diabetes.

By predicting these risks, doctors can take proactive measures to prevent or manage these conditions more effectively.

In addition to improving disease prognosis accuracy, AI also has the potential to assist doctors in making treatment decisions.

By analyzing data from clinical trials and research studies, AI algorithms can recommend treatment options based on the specific characteristics of a patient's disease.

This individualized approach helps doctors tailor treatments to each patient's unique needs and maximize their chances of successful outcomes.

Understanding predictive modeling for disease prognosis is crucial in modern healthcare.

With the help of artificial intelligence, doctors are able to make more accurate predictions about a patient's future health outcomes based on their individual characteristics and medical history.

By leveraging the power of AI algorithms, healthcare professionals can develop personalized treatment plans and provide better care for each patient.

So next time you visit your doctor, remember that behind-the-scenes technology like AI may be playing a key role in ensuring your health and well-being.

Understanding Predictive Modeling for Disease Prognosis

Imagine being able to accurately predict your future health outcomes without having to rely on complex algorithms or medical professionals. This is exactly what predictive modeling for disease prognosis aims to achieve.

Through the use of artificial intelligence (AI) and machine learning techniques, predictive models can analyze patient data and provide accurate predictions about the progression of diseases. By examining various factors such as age, gender, lifestyle choices, genetic predispositions, and medical history, these models can estimate the likelihood of developing certain conditions or experiencing specific health outcomes.

The power of predictive modeling lies in its ability to identify patterns and trends within large sets of patient data. AI algorithms can detect subtle correlations between different variables that may not be immediately obvious to human observers. For example, a model might find that individuals with a particular gene variant have a higher risk of developing a certain type of cancer if they also engage in smoking or have a family history of the disease. These insights can help healthcare providers make more informed decisions regarding prevention strategies, early detection methods, and personalized treatment plans.

Analyzing patient data for accurate predictions is just one aspect of predictive modeling for disease prognosis. The ultimate goal is to empower individuals with knowledge about their own health risks so they can take proactive steps towards better outcomes. By understanding their personal risk factors and making informed lifestyle choices, individuals can potentially reduce their chances of developing certain diseases or manage existing conditions more effectively.

In this way, predictive modeling has the potential to revolutionize healthcare by shifting the focus from reactive treatments to proactive prevention strategies.

With advancements in AI technologies and access to vast amounts of medical data, we are entering an era where predicting our future health outcomes is becoming increasingly possible. By harnessing the power of predictive modeling and AI algorithms, we can gain valuable insights into our individual risks for various diseases and make informed decisions about our health.

So, imagine having the ability to take charge of your own well-being by leveraging this cutting-edge technology - it's a future that's not so far away.

Analyzing Patient Data for Accurate Predictions

By analyzing your personal health data, you can gain accurate predictions about your future well-being and make informed decisions about your health. With the help of AI and predictive modeling, healthcare professionals are able to analyze vast amounts of patient data to identify patterns and trends that may indicate the likelihood of developing certain diseases or conditions.

By inputting various factors such as age, gender, medical history, lifestyle choices, and genetic information into sophisticated algorithms, these models can generate personalized predictions about an individual's risk for specific illnesses.

To ensure accuracy in these predictions, patient data is carefully analyzed using advanced statistical techniques. Here is a breakdown of how healthcare professionals analyze this data:

- Data collection: Relevant information about patients is collected from various sources such as electronic health records (EHRs), wearable devices, medical imaging results, genetic tests, and lifestyle surveys.

- Data preprocessing: The collected information undergoes preprocessing where it is cleaned and organized to remove any inconsistencies or errors that could affect the accuracy of the predictions.

- Feature selection: Healthcare professionals select the most relevant features from the collected data to train the predictive models. These features could include variables like blood pressure readings, cholesterol levels, family history of diseases, or lifestyle habits.

- Model training and validation: The selected features are used to train machine learning models that learn from historical patient data. These models are then validated using separate datasets to ensure their accuracy before being used for prediction purposes.

By accurately analyzing your personal health data through AI-driven predictive modeling techniques like these, healthcare professionals can provide you with valuable insights into your future well-being. This allows for the development of personalized treatment plans aimed at improving patient outcomes without having to rely solely on trial-and-error approaches.

Personalized Treatment Plans and Improved Patient Outcomes

Through the utilization of advanced data analysis techniques, healthcare professionals can tailor treatment plans to individual patients, resulting in improved outcomes. By analyzing patient data and using predictive modeling algorithms, doctors can identify the most effective treatments for each specific case. This personalized approach takes into account factors such as genetic predispositions, medical history, lifestyle choices, and even personal preferences.

As a result, patients receive treatments that are specifically designed to address their unique needs and circumstances. Personalized treatment plans have the potential to significantly improve patient outcomes. Traditional one-size-fits-all approaches may not always be effective for everyone.

By customizing treatment plans based on individual characteristics and risk factors, healthcare providers can optimize the chances of successful outcomes.

For example, a patient with a higher genetic risk of developing certain diseases could benefit from more aggressive preventive measures or targeted therapies. On the other hand, individuals who are less likely to respond well to standard treatments can be spared unnecessary side effects by receiving alternative options.

As we look towards the future of AI in disease prognosis, it is clear that personalized treatment plans will continue to play a crucial role in improving patient outcomes. With advancements in technology and access to larger datasets, AI algorithms will become even more accurate at predicting disease progression and response to different interventions. This will enable healthcare professionals to make better-informed decisions when creating tailored treatment plans for their patients.

By leveraging these capabilities, we can expect further advancements in medical care that prioritize individual needs and maximize positive health outcomes without sacrificing efficiency or quality of care. This will ultimately lead to improved patient satisfaction and overall well-being, as healthcare professionals will be able to provide more personalized and targeted treatments based on a comprehensive understanding of each patient's unique circumstances and medical history.

By integrating data-driven insights into treatment planning, healthcare providers can identify potential risks, predict disease progression, and customize interventions accordingly. This holistic approach to healthcare will revolutionize the industry by ensuring that patients receive the most effective and efficient treatments, ultimately leading to better health outcomes and a higher standard of care.

The Future of AI in Disease Prognosis

In the future, doctors may be able to use advanced data analysis techniques to accurately forecast how a patient's condition will progress and tailor their treatment plan accordingly. For example, a patient with early-stage lung cancer could have their tumor growth rate predicted using AI algorithms, allowing doctors to determine the optimal timing for surgery or targeted therapies.

By accurately predicting how a disease will progress, doctors can intervene at the most opportune moment, maximizing the chances of successful treatment and minimizing unnecessary interventions. This personalized approach can lead to improved patient outcomes and quality of life.

AI algorithms can analyze vast amounts of patient data, including genetic information, medical history, lifestyle factors, and even social determinants of health. By considering all these variables together, AI systems can identify patterns and correlations that may not be apparent to human doctors alone.

This comprehensive analysis allows for more accurate predictions about disease progression and response to different treatments. It empowers doctors with valuable insights that can influence their decision-making process.

With further advancements in AI technology, we may see an integration of real-time monitoring devices that continuously collect patient data. Imagine wearable sensors that track vital signs or smart home devices that monitor sleep patterns or environmental factors. These continuous streams of data could further enhance disease prognosis by providing an up-to-date picture of a patient's health status.

The combination of predictive modeling and real-time monitoring has the potential to revolutionize healthcare delivery by enabling proactive intervention rather than reactive treatment. Ultimately, this could result in better management of chronic conditions and improved overall health outcomes for patients.

The future holds great promise for leveraging AI in disease prognosis. By accurately forecasting disease progression through advanced data analysis techniques and integrating real-time monitoring capabilities, doctors will be able to tailor personalized treatment plans with precision. This approach has the potential to revolutionize healthcare delivery by improving patient outcomes while minimizing unnecessary interventions.

Frequently Asked Questions

How does artificial intelligence in healthcare impact the cost of medical treatment?
Artificial intelligence in healthcare has a positive impact on the cost of medical treatment. It helps streamline processes, improve efficiency, and reduce errors, ultimately leading to lower costs for patients and healthcare providers.

What are the potential ethical concerns surrounding the use of predictive modeling for disease prognosis?
One potential ethical concern is the possibility of false positives in disease prognosis, leading to unnecessary stress and interventions. For example, imagine receiving a prediction of a fatal disease only to later find out it was incorrect.

How can analyzing patient data using AI algorithms improve the accuracy of disease predictions?
Analyzing patient data using AI algorithms can improve disease predictions by identifying patterns and correlations that humans may miss. This helps in accurate diagnosis and treatment planning, leading to better outcomes for patients.

Are there any limitations or risks associated with personalized treatment plans based on AI-generated prognostic models?

Personalized treatment plans based on AI-generated prognostic models have limitations and risks. These include potential inaccuracies in predictions, reliance on historical data, lack of human intuition, and ethical concerns regarding privacy and bias.

What are some potential challenges and barriers to implementing AI in disease prognosis on a large scale in the future?
Challenges and barriers to implementing AI in disease prognosis on a large scale include data quality, ethical concerns, and lack of trust. These obstacles could hinder the widespread adoption of AI in healthcare.

Conclusion

In conclusion, you now have a better understanding of how artificial intelligence (AI) and predictive modeling play a crucial role in disease prognosis.

By analyzing vast amounts of patient data, AI algorithms can accurately predict the course of a disease and help medical professionals develop personalized treatment plans. This ultimately leads to improved patient outcomes and more effective healthcare.

Now, you might be thinking that relying on AI for such important decisions takes away the human touch from healthcare. But let me assure you, AI is not meant to replace doctors or nurses. Instead, it acts as a powerful tool that enhances their capabilities and helps them make informed decisions based on data-driven insights.

Imagine being a patient diagnosed with a life-threatening illness. You want the best possible chance at survival and recovery. With AI technology assisting in your prognosis, doctors can offer you tailored treatment options that are most likely to work for you specifically. This level of personalization gives hope and reassurance in what may seem like an overwhelming situation.

So, while some may argue that relying on machines seems impersonal, we must remember the ultimate goal: improving patient outcomes and saving lives. By embracing AI in disease prognosis, we can harness its power to revolutionize healthcare and provide individuals with the best possible care they deserve.

AI-Driven Drug Discovery and Personalized Medicine

Imagine a world where finding new treatments for diseases is not a slow and arduous process but rather an accelerated journey. Thanks to artificial intelligence, that world is becoming a reality.

AI plays a crucial role in drug discovery by analyzing vast amounts of data to identify potential drug candidates. By sifting through mountains of information from scientific literature, clinical trials, and genetic databases, AI algorithms can pinpoint molecules that have the potential to be effective drugs.

This data analysis saves researchers valuable time and resources by narrowing down the pool of possibilities and allowing them to focus on the most promising leads.

Key Takeaways

- AI is revolutionizing drug discovery and personalized medicine.
- AI algorithms analyze biological and chemical data to speed up the early stages of drug discovery.
- AI reduces costs associated with failed experiments by predicting compound efficacy and toxicity rates.
- Personalized medicine tailors treatments to individual patients, taking into account their genetic makeup and lifestyle.

The Role of Artificial Intelligence in Drug Discovery

Artificial intelligence, or AI, is revolutionizing the field of drug discovery by employing advanced algorithms and machine learning to analyze vast amounts of biological data and identify potential new drugs with enhanced precision. Traditional methods of drug discovery can take years or even decades to find a viable candidate, but with AI, this process is being significantly accelerated.

By analyzing complex patterns in biological data, AI algorithms can quickly identify molecules that have the potential to interact with specific disease targets.

AI-driven drug discovery starts by collecting large amounts of data from various sources such as scientific literature, research databases, and clinical trials. This data is then processed and analyzed using sophisticated algorithms that can detect patterns and relationships between different variables. These algorithms are trained on existing drug compounds and their known interactions to develop predictive models for future drug discovery.

The use of AI in drug discovery not only speeds up the process but also increases the chances of finding successful treatments. By analyzing vast amounts of data in a short amount of time, AI can identify potential drugs that would have been missed using traditional methods. This has the potential to greatly improve patient outcomes by providing targeted therapies that are tailored to an individual's unique genetic makeup and disease profile.

With AI-driven drug discovery leading the way, we are entering an era where personalized medicine becomes a reality.

By employing advanced algorithms and machine learning techniques, AI has transformed how drugs are discovered. The ability to analyze vast amounts of biological data has allowed researchers to identify potential new drugs with unprecedented precision. With AI accelerating the drug development process, we can expect faster breakthroughs in medicine without sacrificing quality or safety standards.

Accelerating the Drug Development Process with AI

Imagine how quickly you could revolutionize the way new treatments are developed if you could harness an unstoppable force of innovation and efficiency. Well, that's exactly what artificial intelligence (AI) is doing in the field of drug development. By leveraging AI algorithms and machine learning techniques, researchers can accelerate the drug development process like never before.

AI has the ability to analyze vast amounts of data, identify patterns, and make predictions that would take humans years to accomplish. With AI, scientists can now sift through massive databases of chemical compounds and predict their potential efficacy or toxicity, significantly speeding up the early stages of drug discovery.

One key area where AI is making a tremendous impact is in identifying potential drug candidates through data analysis. With traditional methods, scientists had to manually screen thousands or even millions of compounds to find those with desirable properties for treating a specific disease. This laborious process often took years and was prone to human error. However, with AI-driven approaches, researchers can train algorithms on existing data from successful drugs and use them to predict which compounds are likely to have similar therapeutic effects. This not only saves time but also increases the chances of finding promising candidates early in the drug development pipeline.

By harnessing the power of AI, researchers are able to accelerate the drug development process by leaps and bounds. The ability to quickly identify potential drug candidates through data analysis allows scientists to focus their efforts on compounds that show promise from the start. This targeted approach reduces costs associated with failed experiments and increases overall efficiency in bringing new treatments to patients who need them most.

With this newfound speed and precision, we're entering an era where personalized medicine tailored specifically for individual patients becomes a reality – all thanks to AI-driven drug discovery.

Transition into 'Identifying Potential Drug Candidates Through Data Analysis': Now that you understand how AI is accelerating the drug development process by predicting compound efficacy and toxicity rates rapidly...

Identifying Potential Drug Candidates through Data Analysis

With the power of data analysis, you can swiftly pinpoint potential drug candidates that hold the key to unlocking new treatments. By analyzing vast amounts of biological and chemical data, AI algorithms can identify molecules that have the potential to interact with specific disease targets and produce therapeutic effects.

This enables researchers to narrow down their focus and prioritize the most promising drug candidates for further investigation. Data analysis plays a crucial role in this process by sifting through complex datasets and identifying patterns or relationships that may not be immediately apparent to human researchers.

Through machine learning techniques, AI systems can learn from existing data about successful drugs and make predictions about the effectiveness of new compounds. This accelerates the drug discovery process by reducing the time and resources required for experimental testing.

By leveraging the power of data analysis, researchers are able to identify potential drug candidates more efficiently than ever before. This opens up new possibilities for developing innovative treatments that could revolutionize healthcare.

In the next section, we will explore how personalized medicine takes these advancements even further by tailoring treatments to individual patients' unique characteristics and needs.

Personalized Medicine: Tailoring Treatments to Individual Patients

By tailoring treatments to your unique characteristics and needs, researchers are revolutionizing healthcare and providing personalized care that can genuinely improve your life. Personalized medicine takes into account factors such as your genetic makeup, lifestyle choices, and environmental influences to develop a treatment plan that is tailored specifically for you.

Here are four ways in which personalized medicine is changing the landscape of healthcare:

- Precision diagnosis: With personalized medicine, doctors can use advanced technologies to identify diseases at an early stage by analyzing your genetic markers. This allows for more accurate diagnoses and enables doctors to intervene before the disease progresses further.

- Targeted therapies: Personalized medicine allows for targeted therapies that focus on specific molecular targets in your body. By identifying the underlying causes of diseases at a molecular level, doctors can develop treatments that directly address these causes, leading to more effective outcomes with fewer side effects.

- Predictive risk assessment: Through personalized medicine, doctors can assess your individual risk factors for developing certain conditions or diseases based on genetic predispositions and other factors. This information helps them create preventive strategies tailored to minimize your risks and promote overall well-being.

- Treatment monitoring: Personalized medicine also involves regular monitoring of treatment progress using biomarkers unique to each patient. This allows doctors to make real-time adjustments to the treatment plan based on how you respond, ensuring optimal results throughout the course of therapy.

By tailoring treatments to each patient's unique characteristics and needs, researchers are revolutionizing healthcare and providing personalized care that can genuinely improve lives. Personalized medicine takes into account factors such as genetic makeup, lifestyle choices, and environmental influences when developing treatment plans specifically for individuals like yourself.

Here are four ways in which personalized medicine is changing healthcare:

1. Precision diagnosis: Advanced technologies allow doctors to analyze genetic markers early on, enabling accurate diagnoses before diseases progress further.

2. Targeted therapies: By identifying underlying causes at a molecular level, personalized medicine develops treatments that directly address these causes, resulting in more effective outcomes with fewer side effects.

3. Predictive risk assessment: Personalized medicine assesses individual risk factors based on genetic predispositions and other factors, allowing doctors to create tailored preventive strategies.

4. Treatment monitoring: Regular monitoring of treatment progress using unique biomarkers for each patient allows real-time adjustments to optimize results throughout therapy.

With the benefits of AI in improving healthcare outcomes, personalized medicine is just one aspect of how technology is revolutionizing patient care.

The Benefits of AI in Improving Healthcare Outcomes

The integration of artificial intelligence into healthcare has significantly enhanced patient outcomes, revolutionizing the way medical professionals diagnose and treat various conditions. AI-driven technologies have the ability to analyze large amounts of data quickly and accurately, allowing for more precise diagnoses and treatment plans tailored to individual patients.

By utilizing machine learning algorithms, AI can identify patterns and predict disease progression, helping doctors make informed decisions about potential treatments.

One of the main benefits of AI in improving healthcare outcomes is its ability to detect diseases at an early stage. With AI-powered tools, such as image recognition software or genetic sequencing algorithms, doctors can identify subtle signs or genetic markers that may indicate a higher risk for certain diseases. This early detection allows for interventions before symptoms even appear, increasing the chances of successful treatment and long-term management.

Another advantage is that AI can assist in predicting how a patient will respond to different treatments. By analyzing data from similar cases and considering factors such as genetics, lifestyle choices, and environmental influences, AI algorithms can provide personalized recommendations on which medications or therapies are likely to be most effective for a specific individual. This not only saves time but also helps avoid trial-and-error approaches that can lead to adverse reactions or ineffective treatments.

The integration of artificial intelligence into healthcare has brought numerous benefits that improve patient outcomes. From early disease detection to personalized treatment plans, AI-driven technologies offer medical professionals valuable insights and tools for delivering more precise care.

As technology continues to advance in this field, we can expect further advancements that will continue to enhance our understanding of diseases and improve overall healthcare outcomes for individuals around the world.

Frequently Asked Questions

How does artificial intelligence help in identifying potential drug candidates through data analysis?

Artificial intelligence helps you identify potential drug candidates by analyzing data. It uses advanced algorithms to sift through vast amounts of information, finding patterns and correlations that humans might miss.

What are the challenges faced in the drug development process that AI can help overcome?

AI can help overcome challenges in the drug development process like high costs, lengthy timelines, and low success rates. It enables faster data analysis, prediction of drug efficacy, and identification of potential safety concerns.

Can personalized medicine really tailor treatments to individual patients?

Yes, personalized medicine can truly tailor treatments to individual patients. In fact, studies show that it has the potential to reduce adverse drug reactions by 40% and improve patient outcomes by 56%.

What are some specific examples of how AI has improved healthcare outcomes?

AI has improved healthcare outcomes in various ways. For example, it has helped in diagnosing diseases more accurately and quickly, predicting patient outcomes, optimizing treatment plans, and even discovering new drugs.

Are there any ethical concerns surrounding the use of AI in drug discovery and personalized medicine?

Ethical concerns surrounding AI in drug discovery and personalized medicine include data privacy, bias in algorithms, and the potential for loss of human control. These issues need to be addressed to ensure responsible and equitable use of AI in healthcare.

Conclusion

In conclusion, you've now seen how Artificial Intelligence (AI) is revolutionizing the field of drug discovery and personalized medicine. With AI's ability to analyze vast amounts of data and identify potential drug candidates, researchers are able to speed up the development process and bring life-saving treatments to patients faster than ever before.

It's like having a super-powered detective on your side, sifting through mountains of information to uncover hidden gems that could save lives. But AI doesn't stop there. It also plays a crucial role in personalized medicine, tailoring treatments to individual patients based on their unique genetic makeup and medical history.

Imagine having a personal chef who knows exactly what ingredients you need for optimal health and creates customized meals just for you. That's what AI does in healthcare – it takes into account all the factors that make you who you are and helps doctors prescribe treatments that are specifically tailored to your needs.

In short, AI-driven drug discovery and personalized medicine hold immense promise for improving healthcare outcomes. They have the potential to transform the way we develop drugs, saving time, money, and ultimately lives.

So, embrace this new era of medical innovation – with AI by our side, we can unlock a world of possibilities in healthcare that were once unimaginable.

CHAPTER 10: AI IN SOCIETY

Impact of AI on Jobs and the Economy

Are you worried about how artificial intelligence (AI) will affect jobs and the economy? AI is rapidly transforming industries and reshaping the workforce, leading to both concerns and opportunities.

In this section, we will explore the impact of AI on jobs and the economy, so you can understand how this technology may shape your future.

Imagine a world where machines can perform tasks that were once exclusive to humans. This is becoming a reality with the rise of AI.

While some fear that AI will lead to massive job losses and unemployment, it's important to consider both sides of the coin. On one hand, AI has the potential to automate certain jobs, such as repetitive tasks or data analysis, which could result in displacement for some workers. On the other hand, new job opportunities are also emerging as businesses adopt AI technologies and require professionals who can develop, implement, and maintain these systems.

By understanding how AI impacts jobs and the economy at a fundamental level, you can better navigate this technological revolution with confidence.

Key Takeaways

- AI is rapidly transforming industries and reshaping the workforce.
- AI has the potential to automate certain jobs, leading to displacement for some workers.
- New job opportunities are also emerging as businesses adopt AI technologies.
- Workers need to adapt their skills and work alongside AI to stay relevant in the job market.

The Role of AI in Job Automation

AI's role in job automation is causing quite a stir, as it's taking over tasks that were once done by humans, leading to concerns about unemployment rates and the future of work.

With the advancements in artificial intelligence technology, machines are now able to perform complex tasks that were previously only possible for human workers. This has led to increased efficiency and productivity in many industries, but it has also raised questions about the impact on employment.

As AI continues to evolve, there is a growing fear that jobs will be lost or displaced. Many routine and repetitive tasks can already be automated with AI, such as data entry or customer service chatbots. This means that some jobs may become obsolete as machines take over these roles. However, it's important to note that while certain jobs may disappear, new opportunities will arise as well. The key is for workers to adapt their skills and find ways to work alongside AI rather than being replaced by it.

The potential job losses and displacements caused by AI should not be taken lightly. It's crucial for individuals and society as a whole to prepare for this shift in the labor market. Education and training programs should focus on developing skills that are complementary to AI technology, such as critical thinking, creativity, and problem-solving abilities. By doing so, we can ensure that humans remain relevant in an increasingly automated world.

The role of AI in job automation is transforming industries and raising concerns about unemployment rates. While some jobs may be lost or displaced due to advancements in artificial intelligence technology, new opportunities will also emerge. It's important for individuals to adapt their skills and embrace lifelong learning in order to thrive alongside AI rather than being replaced by it.

Transitioning into the next section about potential job losses and displacements without explicitly stating 'step', we must address how this shift requires us all to prepare for changes in the labor market.

Potential Job Losses and Displacements

With the rise of artificial intelligence, there's no denying that some jobs will be lost or changed in ways we might not expect. While AI has the potential to greatly improve efficiency and productivity, it also poses a threat to certain industries and job roles.

Here are three ways in which AI could lead to job losses and displacements:

- Automation of repetitive tasks: AI systems can quickly learn and perform routine tasks that were previously done by humans. This includes data entry, basic customer service interactions, and even certain medical diagnoses. As AI continues to advance, more jobs that involve repetitive tasks may become automated, leading to potential layoffs for workers in these fields.

- Advanced robotics replacing manual labor: With advancements in robotics technology, machines are becoming increasingly capable of performing physical labor tasks that were traditionally done by humans. This includes jobs like manufacturing assembly lines, warehouse operations, and even some construction work. As companies adopt more advanced robots powered by AI algorithms, workers in these industries may face displacement as their roles are taken over by machines.

- Intelligent algorithms replacing knowledge-based professions: AI-powered algorithms have shown remarkable capabilities in analyzing vast amounts of data and making complex decisions based on patterns and trends. This poses a threat to jobs that require extensive knowledge or expertise in areas such as finance, law, journalism, and even medicine. As AI algorithms continue to improve their decision-making abilities, professionals in these fields may see a decrease in demand for their services.

As we explore the potential job losses caused by AI advancements, it is crucial to acknowledge that this technology also creates new opportunities for employment. Transitioning into the next section about 'new job opportunities created by AI,' we can discuss how individuals can adapt their skills and embrace emerging roles within this evolving landscape without being left behind. It is crucial for individuals to proactively acquire new skills and embrace emerging roles within this evolving landscape to avoid being left behind in the rapidly changing job market.

New Job Opportunities Created by AI

The future is ripe with exciting possibilities as AI opens up doors to diverse and rewarding career paths. With the advancement of AI technology, new job opportunities are emerging in various sectors.

One such sector is data analysis and interpretation. AI systems can process large amounts of data in a fraction of the time it would take a human, allowing businesses to gain valuable insights and make informed decisions. As a result, there is an increasing demand for professionals who can understand and extract meaningful information from these vast datasets.

Another area where AI is creating new job opportunities is in the field of programming and development. As AI becomes more sophisticated, there is a need for skilled individuals who can design, build, and maintain these intelligent systems. From developing algorithms that power machine learning models to creating user-friendly interfaces for AI applications, programmers are at the forefront of this technological revolution. This opens up avenues for those interested in pursuing careers in software engineering or artificial intelligence research.

Furthermore, as AI automates certain tasks, it also creates opportunities for individuals to focus on higher-level skills that require creativity and critical thinking. Jobs that involve complex problem-solving or strategic decision-making cannot be easily automated by AI systems. Therefore, there will always be a need for professionals who possess these unique human qualities. Whether it's coming up with innovative marketing strategies or providing personalized customer experiences, individuals with creative thinking abilities will continue to thrive alongside AI technology.

The rise of AI brings forth a multitude of new job opportunities across various industries. From data analysis to programming and development, there are numerous career paths waiting to be explored. Moreover, as automation takes over mundane tasks, individuals with higher-level skills like creativity and critical thinking will find themselves even more valuable in the workforce. The future looks promising as we embrace the potential of AI while enhancing productivity through its integration into our daily lives without sacrificing our unique human capabilities.

Enhancing Productivity with AI

To boost efficiency and output, you can harness the power of AI to streamline processes and maximize productivity. AI technologies, such as machine learning algorithms, natural language processing, and robotic process automation, can automate repetitive tasks, allowing employees to focus on more strategic and value-added activities.

For example, AI-powered chatbots can handle customer inquiries and provide instant responses, freeing up human agents to handle more complex issues. By automating routine tasks through AI, companies can significantly increase their overall productivity.

In addition to automation, AI can also help companies make better decisions by analyzing vast amounts of data in real-time. With advanced analytics capabilities, AI systems can identify patterns and trends that humans may miss. This enables businesses to make data-driven decisions quickly and accurately.

For instance, predictive analytics models powered by AI algorithms can forecast demand fluctuations or identify potential risks in supply chains. By leveraging the power of AI in decision-making processes, companies can optimize their operations and achieve higher levels of productivity.

As we explore how AI enhances productivity, it is important to consider the potential impact on jobs and the economy as a whole. While some may fear that increased reliance on AI will lead to job losses, it is crucial to find a balance between embracing technological advancements and preserving human employment opportunities.

The key lies in reskilling workers for jobs that require uniquely human skills, such as creativity, critical thinking, empathy, and problem-solving abilities – areas where machines still struggle. By combining the strengths of humans with the capabilities of AI technologies, we can create a future where both productivity gains and job growth go hand in hand.

Balancing the Impact of AI on Jobs and the Economy

Finding a balance between embracing AI advancements and preserving human employment opportunities is crucial for ensuring the future of jobs and economic stability. While AI has the potential to automate tasks and increase efficiency, it's important to consider its impact on job displacement. Here are four key points to keep in mind:

- Upskilling and reskilling: As AI technology evolves, some jobs may become obsolete. However, this also presents an opportunity for workers to acquire new skills that are in demand. By investing in training programs and providing resources for upskilling and reskilling, individuals can adapt to changing job requirements and remain employable.

- Job creation through innovation: Although certain roles may be replaced by AI, new job opportunities can emerge as industries evolve. Innovation brought about by AI can lead to the creation of entirely new sectors, driving economic growth and generating employment prospects in areas we might not have anticipated.

- Collaborative approach: Instead of viewing AI as a threat, organizations should adopt a collaborative approach where humans work alongside machines. By leveraging the strengths of both humans and AI systems, businesses can enhance productivity while maintaining human involvement in decision-making processes that require creativity, empathy, and critical thinking.

- Social safety nets: Governments play a crucial role in addressing the impact of AI on jobs and the economy. Implementing social safety nets such as unemployment benefits or Universal Basic Income (UBI) can provide support during periods of transition or when jobs are displaced due to automation.

By finding this delicate balance between embracing technological advancements while considering the well-being of workers, society can harness the benefits of AI without leaving anyone behind. It's essential to create an environment where humans continue to contribute their unique skills while benefiting from increased productivity brought about by artificial intelligence technologies.

Frequently Asked Questions

How does AI impact the job market in terms of job automation?

AI impacts the job market by automating tasks previously done by humans. This increases efficiency, but also raises concerns about job loss. Will AI replace your job next?

What are the potential job losses and displacements caused by AI?

AI has the potential to cause job losses and displacements by automating tasks that were previously done by humans. This could lead to some jobs becoming obsolete and workers needing to find new roles or acquire new skills.

Are there new job opportunities being created as a result of AI advancements? Absolutely! AI advancements have opened up a world of new job opportunities. From AI trainers and data scientists to automation specialists, there are plenty of exciting roles emerging in various industries.

How can AI enhance productivity in different industries?
AI can enhance productivity in different industries by automating repetitive tasks, analyzing big data for insights, and making accurate predictions. You'll see increased efficiency, cost savings, and improved decision-making processes as AI takes over certain aspects of work.

What measures are being taken to balance the impact of AI on jobs and the overall economy?
To balance the impact of AI on jobs and the economy, organizations are investing in reskilling programs to equip workers with new skills. Government policies are being developed to address potential job displacement while fostering innovation and economic growth.

Conclusion

In conclusion, AI is like a double-edged sword that can both threaten and empower our workforce. It has the potential to revolutionize industries, streamline processes, and enhance productivity. However, it also poses a significant risk of job losses and displacements.

Imagine a world where robots seamlessly take over mundane tasks, freeing up humans to focus on more complex and creative endeavors. Picture a future where AI-powered systems assist doctors in diagnosing diseases faster and with greater accuracy, or where self-driving cars reduce traffic accidents and congestion. These are just glimpses of the immense potential that AI holds for our society.

But let us not forget about those who may suffer from these advancements—the workers whose jobs are at risk of being automated away. We must strive to find ways to retrain and reskill them for new roles created by AI. By striking a delicate balance between harnessing the power of AI for economic growth while ensuring equitable opportunities for all, we can navigate the impact of AI on jobs and the economy together.

So, let's embrace this technological wave with open arms but also with mindful consideration for its consequences. By doing so, we can shape an inclusive future where both humans and machines coexist harmoniously, driving progress in unimaginable ways. The choice is ours – will we seize the opportunity or let it slip through our fingers?

Ethical Considerations and Challenges in AI Development and Deployment

Are you worried about the ethical considerations and challenges surrounding AI development and deployment? You might be thinking, 'But I'm not a tech expert! How can I possibly understand these complex concepts?'

Well, fear not! In this section, we will break down the ethical concerns related to AI, so you can grasp the impact it has on society and individuals like yourself.

Now, you may be wondering why you should even care about this topic. After all, AI seems like something only scientists and engineers need to worry about. But here's the thing - AI is already deeply integrated into our daily lives. From personalized recommendations on streaming platforms to voice assistants that respond to our every command, AI algorithms are making decisions that directly affect us.

And when these algorithms are biased or discriminatory, they can perpetuate inequalities and reinforce harmful stereotypes. So, it's crucial for everyone to understand the potential consequences of unchecked AI development and deployment.

Key Takeaways

- AI algorithms can perpetuate inequalities and stereotypes if they are biased or discriminatory, so it is crucial to be aware of these consequences and actively work to eliminate biases.
- Privacy is a major ethical consideration in AI development, and balancing the use of data for beneficial purposes with safeguarding privacy is a challenge that requires strict policies and regulations.
- Fairness, transparency, and accountability should be prioritized in designing and training AI systems, and users should have control over their own data and be informed about its use by AI systems.
- Collaboration between different disciplines and engagement of diverse stakeholders, including marginalized communities, are important for creating inclusive and responsible AI systems.

Impact on Society and Individuals

AI development and deployment can have profound consequences on society and individuals, leaving you feeling both awestruck by its potential and concerned about the ethical implications. On one hand, AI has the power to revolutionize industries, improve efficiency, and enhance our daily lives in ways we never thought possible. It can assist doctors in diagnosing diseases, help self-driving cars navigate safely on roads, and even provide personalized recommendations for movies or music. However, with this immense power also comes great responsibility.

One of the biggest concerns is the impact of AI on jobs. As AI technology advances, there's a fear that many jobs will become automated, leading to unemployment and inequality. While some argue that new jobs will be created as a result of AI advancements, others worry about the speed at which job displacement may occur. This raises questions about retraining programs for those affected by automation and ensuring fair distribution of wealth in a society increasingly driven by AI.

Another ethical consideration is privacy. With the proliferation of smart devices connected to the internet, AI algorithms are constantly collecting data about us - from our online activities to our shopping habits. While this data can be used to improve user experiences or target advertising more effectively, it also raises concerns about surveillance and invasion of privacy. Striking a balance between using these insights for beneficial purposes while safeguarding individual privacy rights remains an ongoing challenge.

While AI development offers incredible opportunities for societal advancement and personal convenience, it also poses significant ethical challenges that must be addressed proactively. The next section will explore one such challenge: bias in AI algorithms - an issue that requires careful consideration as we strive to create fairer and more inclusive technologies without compromising their potential benefits.

Bias in AI Algorithms

The glaring issue of bias in AI algorithms is like a giant elephant in the room that can't be ignored. As humans, we have our own biases and prejudices, and unfortunately, these biases can seep into the development and deployment of AI systems.

When training AI algorithms, developers use large datasets to teach the system how to make decisions or predictions. However, if these datasets contain biased information or reflect societal prejudices, the AI system will learn and perpetuate those biases.

This bias can have significant consequences for society and individuals. For example, biased AI algorithms could lead to unfair treatment in hiring processes or loan applications. If an algorithm is more likely to reject applicants from certain ethnic backgrounds or unfairly favor one gender over another, it perpetuates existing inequalities instead of promoting fairness and equal opportunities.

To address this issue, developers need to be aware of their own biases and take steps to ensure that their datasets are diverse and representative of all groups in society. They should also regularly test their algorithms for bias by analyzing the outcomes they produce across different demographic groups. By actively working towards reducing bias in AI algorithms, we can create more equitable systems that benefit everyone.

Now let's transition into discussing privacy concerns related to AI development and deployment. While bias is a pressing concern, it isn't the only ethical consideration surrounding AI technology. Privacy concerns play a crucial role in shaping how AI systems are developed and used.

Privacy Concerns

Protecting your personal information and ensuring your privacy is a top concern when it comes to integrating AI technology into our daily lives. With the increasing use of AI in various aspects of our lives, such as virtual assistants, smart home devices, and online shopping platforms, it's essential to address the privacy concerns associated with these advancements.

Here are three key reasons why privacy is crucial in the context of AI:

1. Data breaches: When AI systems collect and analyze large amounts of personal data, there's always a risk of that data being compromised. Cybercriminals may target this valuable information for malicious purposes, leading to identity theft or financial fraud.
2. Surveillance concerns: As AI-powered surveillance technology becomes more prevalent, there are growing concerns about invasion of privacy. Facial recognition systems and video monitoring can potentially track individuals without their knowledge or consent, raising serious ethical questions about how this data is used.
3. Manipulation and discrimination: Another significant concern with AI technology is its potential for manipulation and discrimination. If algorithms have access to personal information like race, gender, or religion, they may inadvertently perpetuate bias or stereotypes. This can lead to unfair treatment or exclusion based on sensitive characteristics.

Safeguarding personal data and addressing these concerns requires robust privacy policies and regulations that hold companies accountable for protecting user information. By implementing strict security measures, transparent data practices, and giving users control over their own data through informed consent mechanisms, we can ensure that AI technologies respect individual privacy rights while still delivering valuable services.

Now let's explore how safeguarding personal data plays a vital role in mitigating these risks associated with the integration of AI technology into our daily lives.

Safeguarding Personal Data

To ensure the safety of your personal data, it's important to understand that 90% of all data breaches are caused by human error. This means that even with advanced technology and security measures in place, mistakes made by individuals can still lead to the compromise of your sensitive information.

It could be as simple as an employee clicking on a malicious link or accidentally sharing confidential data with unauthorized parties. Therefore, organizations must prioritize training their staff on best practices for handling personal data and implementing strict protocols to minimize human errors.

One way to safeguard your personal data is through encryption. Encryption involves converting your information into a code that can only be deciphered with the correct key. By encrypting your data, even if it gets intercepted or stolen, it would be useless without the decryption key. This provides an extra layer of protection against unauthorized access and ensures that only those who have the proper authorization can view and use your sensitive information.

In addition to encryption, organizations should also implement robust access controls to protect personal data from unauthorized users. This involves assigning unique usernames and passwords to individuals based on their roles and responsibilities within the organization. With proper access controls in place, only authorized personnel will have access to specific sets of data relevant to their job functions. This helps prevent accidental or intentional misuse of personal data by limiting exposure to a select few individuals who are deemed trustworthy.

By taking these measures to safeguard personal data, organizations can better protect you from potential privacy breaches or misuse of your sensitive information. However, ensuring the safety of personal data is just one aspect of ethical responsibilities in AI development and deployment. Next, let's explore how AI developers should also consider other ethical considerations such as fairness, transparency, and accountability when creating AI systems for public use without compromising user privacy. This includes ensuring that AI systems are designed and trained in a way that avoids bias and discrimination, and that the decision-making processes of AI algorithms are transparent and explainable. Additionally, developers should establish mechanisms for accountability, such as clear guidelines for system behavior and regular auditing to identify and rectify any ethical issues that may arise.

Ethical Responsibilities in AI Development and Deployment

You need to ensure that AI systems are designed and trained in a fair, transparent, and accountable manner, while also prioritizing user privacy. It is crucial to consider the potential biases that may be embedded in AI algorithms and data sets. This means actively working to eliminate any unfair or discriminatory outcomes that could arise from the use of AI.

Additionally, transparency is key in ensuring that users understand how AI systems make decisions and what data they are using to do so. By providing clear explanations and making information easily accessible, you can build trust with users.

To fulfill your ethical responsibilities in AI development and deployment, it is important to prioritize user privacy. This involves implementing robust security measures to protect personal data from unauthorized access or misuse. Users should have control over their own data and be informed about how it will be used by AI systems. It is essential to obtain proper consent before collecting any personal information and to handle the data with care throughout its lifecycle.

In order to meet these ethical obligations, you should actively engage with diverse stakeholders during the development process. Seek input from individuals who may be affected by the technology, including those from marginalized communities or groups who may face unique challenges or risks. By involving a range of perspectives early on, you can identify potential issues or unintended consequences before they become problems later down the line.

Collaboration between different disciplines such as computer science, ethics, law, sociology, and psychology can contribute towards creating more inclusive and responsible AI systems for all users.

Key considerations for ethical AI development:

- Eliminating biases: Actively work towards removing unfairness or discrimination in algorithms.
- Transparency: Provide clear explanations of how decisions are made by AI systems.

Ethical responsibilities for protecting user privacy:

- Robust security: Implement strong measures to safeguard personal data.
- User control: Enable users to have control over their own data usage.

By adhering to these principles and engaging in transparent and inclusive practices, you can ensure that AI systems are developed and deployed in an ethical manner. Remember, the responsible development of AI is not just a legal or technical requirement but also an important moral obligation to users and society as a whole.

Frequently Asked Questions

How does the development and deployment of AI impact job security and employment opportunities for individuals?
AI development and deployment can be a double-edged sword for job security. While it creates new opportunities, it also poses a threat by automating tasks traditionally done by humans. It's like a high-speed train that brings both progress and uncertainty to individuals' employment prospects.

What steps are being taken to address the issue of bias in AI algorithms and ensure fair and unbiased decision-making?
Steps are being taken to address bias in AI algorithms and ensure fair decision-making. Researchers are developing techniques to detect and mitigate biases, while organizations are implementing diversity and inclusion practices to improve algorithmic fairness.

How can individuals protect their privacy and personal data in a world increasingly driven by AI technology?
To protect your privacy and personal data in an AI-driven world, you must guard them like a hawk on steroids! Be cautious with what you share online, use strong passwords, and keep up with privacy settings to stay in control.

What are the potential risks associated with the collection and storage of personal data by AI systems, and how can these risks be mitigated?
Potential risks of personal data collection by AI systems include privacy breaches, identity theft, and

discrimination. To mitigate these risks, you can limit the amount of personal information shared, use strong passwords, and regularly monitor your online accounts for any suspicious activity.

What ethical responsibilities do AI developers and deployers have in terms of ensuring transparency and accountability in their algorithms and decision-making processes?

As an AI developer or deployer, you have the ethical responsibility to ensure transparency and accountability in your algorithms and decision-making processes. This means being open about how your AI system works and taking responsibility for any potential biases or errors.

Conclusion

In conclusion, ethical considerations and challenges in AI development and deployment have a significant impact on both society and individuals. The potential biases present in AI algorithms pose a threat to fairness and equality, as they can perpetuate existing social inequalities.

Privacy concerns are also paramount, as personal data is increasingly being collected and used without proper consent or protection.

As an individual, you should be aware of the ethical responsibilities involved in AI development and deployment. It's crucial to advocate for transparency in algorithmic decision-making processes to ensure that biases are identified and addressed. Additionally, safeguarding personal data should be a top priority for both developers and users alike.

For example, let's consider the case of facial recognition technology. This AI tool has gained widespread popularity but has been found to have significant biases against people of color, leading to wrongful identifications by law enforcement agencies. This not only highlights the need for diversity in data sets used for training algorithms but also underscores the importance of rigorous testing procedures before deploying such technologies.

Overall, understanding the ethical implications surrounding AI development is essential for fostering responsible innovation. By addressing bias, privacy concerns, and upholding ethical responsibilities, we can create a more inclusive and equitable future where AI benefits all members of society.

Ensuring Transparency, Fairness, and Accountability in AI Systems

In a world increasingly driven by technology, it is essential to understand the inner workings of AI systems. Ensuring transparency, fairness, and accountability in these systems is paramount for their successful integration into our daily lives. From self-driving cars to virtual assistants, AI has the potential to revolutionize various industries.

But how can we trust something we don't fully comprehend? Transparency lies at the heart of building this trust. By shedding light on the decision-making processes of AI systems, we can gain a deeper understanding of how they reach conclusions or make recommendations. Transparency allows us to peek behind the digital curtain and ensures that these systems are not operating based solely on algorithms hidden away from public scrutiny.

When you know how an AI system arrives at its decisions, you have peace of mind knowing there are no hidden biases or ulterior motives guiding its actions. So, buckle up as we embark on a journey towards understanding the importance of transparency, fairness, and accountability in AI systems and explore how these principles can shape a future where humans coexist harmoniously with intelligent machines.

Key Takeaways

- Transparency, fairness, and accountability in AI systems are important for building public trust and avoiding potential negative consequences.
- Transparent AI systems help users understand how they work and why certain decisions are made, fostering trust and confidence in relying on AI technology.
- Ensuring fairness and accountability in AI helps reduce bias and discrimination, creating an equal playing field for everyone.
- These principles bring benefits to society by increasing trust, enhancing decision-making processes, and ensuring equitable outcomes for all users involved.

The Importance of Transparency in AI Systems

Transparency in AI systems is crucial because it allows us to trust that these technologies are working for us, not against us. When we can see how these systems make decisions and understand the underlying algorithms, it becomes easier to hold them accountable for their actions. Without transparency, AI systems can easily become black boxes, making decisions that affect our lives without any explanation or justification.

Transparency also helps to address concerns about bias and discrimination in AI systems. By being able to see how data is collected and used in these systems, we can identify any biases that may be present and work towards mitigating them. This is especially important when it comes to decision-making processes that impact people's lives, such as hiring or loan approval algorithms. Transparency allows us to ensure fairness and avoid perpetuating existing inequalities.

In addition, transparency fosters collaboration and innovation. When AI systems are transparent, researchers and developers can better understand how they work and build upon existing models. This leads to advancements in the field of AI and encourages the development of more inclusive and ethical technologies. By promoting transparency in AI systems, we can create a future where technology works for everyone and benefits society as a whole.

With transparency established as a foundation for trust in AI systems, we can now delve into the next section: ensuring fairness in AI decision-making. By understanding how decisions are made by these complex algorithms, we can address concerns about bias or discrimination head-on. It's important that we strive for fairness so that everyone has equal opportunities when interacting with AI-powered systems.

Ensuring Fairness in AI Decision-Making

To create a level playing field, AI decision-making must prioritize equity and impartiality. In other words, it's crucial that AI systems make fair and unbiased choices, regardless of an individual's race, gender, or background.

This means ensuring that the algorithms used in these systems are not influenced by any form of bias and do not perpetuate existing social inequalities. By prioritizing fairness in AI decision-making, we can reduce the risk of discriminatory outcomes and promote equal opportunities for all.

One way to ensure fairness in AI decision-making is through data collection and analysis. It is essential to have diverse and representative datasets that accurately reflect the real-world population. Without this diversity, AI systems may inadvertently reinforce existing biases or discriminate against certain groups.

Therefore, collecting data from a wide range of sources and carefully analyzing it can help identify any potential biases present in the dataset. By addressing these biases early on, we can work towards developing AI systems that make decisions without favoring one group over another.

Fairness should be at the core of AI decision-making processes. To achieve this goal, we need to prioritize equity and impartiality when designing algorithms and collecting data for training these systems. By doing so, we can ensure that AI systems make fair decisions that benefit everyone equally.

Moving forward, let's explore how holding AI systems accountable for their actions plays a vital role in building trust with users while avoiding potential harms caused by biased or unfair decisions made by these technologies.

Holding AI Systems Accountable for Their Actions

In order for AI technology to gain trust and avoid potential harm, it's crucial that we hold these systems accountable for their actions. Accountability means that AI systems are responsible for the decisions they make and the consequences that follow.

To achieve this, we need to establish clear guidelines and standards for AI development and deployment. These guidelines should include regular audits of AI systems, ensuring transparency in their decision-making processes, and holding developers responsible for any biases or unfairness in the system's outcomes.

To ensure accountability in AI systems, here are three important steps we can take:

1. Establishing clear rules and regulations: It's essential to have a set of guidelines in place that dictate how AI systems should be developed, tested, deployed, and maintained. These rules should address issues such as bias detection and mitigation techniques, data privacy protection measures, algorithmic transparency requirements, and system monitoring protocols.

2. Conducting regular audits: Just like financial audits ensure compliance with accounting standards, regular audits of AI systems can help identify any biases or unfair practices. Audits should assess the decision-making algorithms used by these systems to check if they align with ethical standards. This process involves scrutinizing training data sets, examining model architectures and parameters, as well as evaluating performance metrics against predefined benchmarks.

3. Holding developers responsible: Developers play a crucial role in building AI systems; therefore, they must be held accountable for any negative impacts caused by their creations. This includes being transparent about how the system works and its limitations upfront while taking responsibility for addressing any unintended consequences or biases that may arise from the technology's usage.

By holding AI systems accountable for their actions through guidelines enforcement, regular audits of system behavior, and developer responsibility-taking measures, we can build trust in AI technology among users while minimizing potential risks associated with biased decisions or unethical practices.

Now let's delve into the next section about building trust in AI technology without compromising its capabilities.

Building Trust in AI Technology

Imagine a world where AI technology is like a trusted companion, guiding you through complex tasks and offering valuable insights without compromising its capabilities. Building trust in AI technology is crucial to ensure its widespread adoption and acceptance.

Trust can be established by ensuring transparency in how AI systems work, making their decision-making processes understandable to the average user. By providing clear explanations of why certain decisions are made or actions are taken, users can have confidence in the reliability and fairness of AI systems.

Another way to build trust in AI technology is by incorporating ethical considerations into its development. AI systems should be designed with fairness and accountability in mind, ensuring that they don't perpetuate biases or discriminate against certain individuals or groups. This means actively addressing issues such as algorithmic bias and taking steps to mitigate them. By doing so, AI technology can gain credibility as an unbiased tool that respects human rights and values.

In addition, building trust requires ongoing monitoring and evaluation of AI systems' performance. Regular audits can help identify any issues or shortcomings in their decision-making processes or outcomes. This allows for continuous improvement and refinement of these systems over time. By proactively addressing concerns and keeping the public informed about the progress being made, trust in AI technology can be strengthened even further.

Ultimately, building trust lays the foundation for reaping the benefits of transparency, fairness, and accountability in AI without compromising innovation or efficiency.

Understanding the importance of building trust in AI technology sets the stage for exploring the numerous benefits that come with ensuring transparency, fairness, and accountability in these systems.

By prioritizing transparency, fairness, and accountability in AI systems, we can unlock the full potential of this technology while fostering public trust and avoiding potential negative consequences.

Benefits of Transparency, Fairness, and Accountability in AI

The benefits of transparency, fairness, and accountability in AI become clear when we consider the potential for increased trust, improved decision-making processes, and reduced bias.

When AI systems are transparent, users can easily understand how they work and why certain decisions are made. This transparency builds trust as people feel more confident in relying on AI technology. They can see that the system is fair and unbiased, which ultimately leads to greater acceptance and adoption.

Furthermore, transparency in AI promotes improved decision-making processes. With access to information about how an AI system operates and the data it uses, individuals can make more informed choices. They can better understand the limitations of the technology and any potential biases present. This empowers users to critically evaluate outputs from AI systems and make their own judgments based on a clearer understanding of the process.

Moreover, ensuring fairness and accountability in AI helps reduce bias within these systems. By implementing measures that prevent discrimination or favoritism based on race, gender, or other protected characteristics, we create a playing field that is equal for everyone. When these biases are minimized or eliminated altogether, AI systems have the potential to provide fairer outcomes across various domains such as hiring processes or loan approvals.

Transparency, fairness, and accountability in AI bring several benefits to society. They foster increased trust by allowing individuals to comprehend how AI makes decisions. These principles also enhance decision-making processes by providing access to critical information about the technology's operation. Lastly, promoting fairness reduces biases within AI systems and ensures equitable outcomes for all users involved.

Frequently Asked Questions

How can transparency in AI systems help prevent biases and discrimination?
Transparency in AI systems is like shining a light on biases and discrimination. By revealing how algorithms work, you can identify and address any unfairness, ensuring that the technology treats everyone equally.

What measures are taken to ensure fairness in the decision-making process of AI systems?
To ensure fairness in AI decision-making, measures like data auditing, diverse training datasets, and algorithmic testing are implemented. These help identify and address biases, promoting a more equitable and unbiased process.

How can AI systems be held accountable for their actions and potential errors?
Hold AI systems accountable by implementing clear guidelines and regulations, conducting regular audits, and establishing mechanisms for reporting errors. You can also ensure transparency by making the decision-making process of AI systems more understandable to users.

What steps are involved in building trust in AI technology among users and stakeholders?
To build trust in AI technology, you need to focus on user and stakeholder confidence. One interesting statistic is that 81% of consumers are concerned about the lack of transparency in AI systems.

Can you provide specific examples of the benefits that transparency, fairness, and accountability bring to AI systems in real-world scenarios?
Transparency, fairness, and accountability in AI systems benefit real-world scenarios. For example, transparent algorithms can help detect bias in hiring processes, ensuring fair opportunities for all candidates. Accountability helps prevent misuse of AI technology, maintaining trust among users and stakeholders.

Conclusion

In conclusion, ensuring transparency, fairness, and accountability in AI systems is crucial in today's technological landscape. By shining a light on the inner workings of AI algorithms and providing clear explanations for their decision-making processes, we empower individuals to understand and trust these systems. This not only improves user experience but also helps prevent biases and discrimination that can arise from opaque AI systems.

Moreover, holding AI systems accountable for their actions is paramount in establishing ethical guidelines and preventing potential harm. Just as humans are held responsible for their behavior, so should AI systems be held to similar standards. This means implementing mechanisms that allow for redress when errors or injustices occur due to automated decisions.

Ultimately, building trust in AI technology is essential for its successful integration into various sectors of society. Transparency allows users to have confidence in the technology they're interacting with, while fairness ensures that no individual or group is unfairly disadvantaged. Accountability holds AI systems responsible for their actions, ensuring that they adhere to ethical principles. By embracing these values, we can harness the full potential of AI while minimizing risks and maximizing benefits – an important step towards a more inclusive and equitable future.

CHAPTER 11: FINAL THOUGHTS

In the modern world, where technology reigns supreme, there is one buzzword that seems to be on everyone's lips: Artificial Intelligence. From self-driving cars to virtual assistants like Siri and Alexa, AI has become an integral part of our daily lives. But what does it really mean to embrace AI? How can we make sense of this complex concept in layman's terms? Look no further, for this final section will delve into the world of AI and guide you through its applications, workings, benefits, and future.

Imagine a world where machines mimic human intelligence with mind-boggling precision. That is the power of Artificial Intelligence. It encompasses a wide range of technologies that enable computers to perform tasks that typically require human intelligence, such as speech recognition, problem-solving, and decision-making.

In today's fast-paced society, AI has permeated various aspects of our lives without us even realizing it. Whether it's the personalized recommendations on streaming platforms or the facial recognition feature on our smartphones, AI is all around us.

Key Takeaways

- Machines becoming more intelligent brings up questions about decision-making and who is accountable for those decisions.
- The rise of AI automation may lead to job displacement, particularly for repetitive tasks.
- It is important to strike a balance between benefiting from AI while avoiding societal inequalities and harm.
- Collaboration among different stakeholders is crucial to successfully navigate the challenges posed by AI.

Applications of AI in Everyday Life

From voice assistants that help you navigate your day to personalized recommendations that enhance your online experiences, AI has seamlessly integrated into various aspects of your everyday life.

Voice assistants like Siri, Alexa, and Google Assistant have become integral parts of our households, allowing us to control smart devices, play music, get weather updates, and even order groceries with just a simple voice command. These AI-powered virtual helpers have made our lives more convenient and efficient.

Moreover, AI is transforming the way we shop online. When you browse through an e-commerce website or scroll through social media platforms, you come across personalized recommendations tailored specifically for you. This is because AI algorithms analyze your browsing history, purchase patterns, and other data points to predict your preferences accurately. By doing so, they ensure that you are presented with products or content that align with your tastes and interests.

In addition to this personalization aspect, AI also plays a significant role in ensuring our safety and security. Facial recognition technology powered by AI helps identify individuals in real-time video surveillance footage or unlock our smartphones using biometrics. Furthermore, advanced machine learning algorithms enable fraud detection systems to identify suspicious activities in financial transactions almost instantly.

With these applications of AI in everyday life becoming increasingly prevalent, it's fascinating to explore how this technology actually works: a simplified explanation about the underlying principles behind artificial intelligence.

(Note: To transition smoothly into the subsequent section without using the word 'step,' we can simply add a sentence like 'Before diving into that explanation,' at the end of the third paragraph.)

How AI Works: A Simplified Explanation

Before we delve into the intricacies of AI, let's start with a simple concept: machine learning. Machine learning is at the core of AI and it works by enabling computers to learn from data and improve their performance over time without being explicitly programmed. It's like teaching a computer to recognize patterns and make predictions based on those patterns.

By using algorithms, machines can analyze large amounts of data, identify trends, and make decisions or recommendations without human intervention. Machine learning relies on training data, which is essentially a set of examples that the computer uses to understand how to perform a specific task.

For example, if we want a machine to recognize images of cats, we would feed it thousands of images labeled as 'cat' so that it can learn what features define a cat. The more diverse and accurate the training data is, the better the machine becomes at recognizing cats in new images.

Once the machine has been trained, it can apply its knowledge to new situations. This is where AI comes into play. By combining machine learning with other technologies such as natural language processing and computer vision, AI systems can perform tasks that were once thought only possible for humans.

From voice assistants like Siri or Alexa to self-driving cars and personalized recommendations on streaming platforms, AI has become an integral part of our everyday lives.

As you can see, understanding how AI works doesn't have to be complicated. It all starts with machine learning and training computers to recognize patterns and make predictions based on data. With this foundation in place, we can now explore the benefits of embracing AI in various aspects of our modern world without skipping a beat.

Benefits of Embracing AI

Discover the incredible advantages you can gain by fully embracing the power of AI in various aspects of your daily life.

One major benefit is increased efficiency and productivity. AI can automate repetitive tasks, freeing up valuable time for more important activities. Whether it's in the workplace or at home, AI can help streamline processes and make your life easier.

Another advantage of embracing AI is improved decision-making. With access to vast amounts of data, AI algorithms can analyze information quickly and accurately, providing you with valuable insights to make informed choices. From personalized recommendations on shopping platforms to medical diagnoses based on symptoms, AI has the potential to revolutionize how we make decisions in both personal and professional settings.

Lastly, embracing AI opens up new possibilities for innovation and creativity. By leveraging machine learning algorithms and predictive analytics, businesses can uncover patterns and trends that were previously unseen. This enables them to develop innovative products and services tailored to customer needs. In addition, AI-powered tools like virtual assistants and language translation services enhance communication across borders, fostering collaboration on a global scale.

As you explore the benefits of embracing AI, it's important to also consider the challenges that come with it. The future of AI presents opportunities for growth but also raises concerns about privacy, ethics, and job displacement. However, by understanding these challenges and actively working towards solutions, we can continue to harness the power of AI while mitigating its potential risks.

The Future of AI: Opportunities and Challenges

The future of AI is a double-edged sword, presenting endless possibilities for advancement while also posing significant challenges that require careful consideration and proactive solutions.

On one hand, AI holds great promise in revolutionizing various industries, from healthcare to transportation. With its ability to process vast amounts of data and make predictions based on patterns, AI can help doctors diagnose diseases more accurately and efficiently, leading to improved patient outcomes. Additionally, self-driving cars equipped with AI technology have the potential to reduce accidents and traffic congestion, making our roads safer and more efficient.

However, along with these opportunities come several challenges that must be addressed. One major concern is the ethical implications of AI. As machines become increasingly intelligent, questions arise about their decision-making capabilities and whether they should be held accountable for their actions. There are also concerns about job displacement as automation powered by AI takes over repetitive tasks traditionally performed by humans. It becomes crucial to strike a balance between embracing the benefits of AI while ensuring that it does not lead to societal inequalities or harm individuals.

To navigate these challenges successfully, collaboration among various stakeholders is essential. Governments need to establish regulations that protect individuals' privacy rights while fostering innovation in the field of AI. Tech companies should prioritize transparency in their algorithms and ensure they are free from bias or discrimination. Society as a whole needs to engage in discussions about the impact of AI on our lives and work towards creating inclusive solutions that benefit everyone.

The future of AI presents both incredible opportunities for advancement as well as significant challenges that demand attention and thoughtful action. By embracing this technology responsibly and addressing ethical concerns proactively, we can harness its potential for positive change while mitigating any negative consequences. The key lies in finding a delicate balance between progress and safeguarding human values so that we can truly embrace AI's transformative power in the modern world.

Frequently Asked Questions

Can AI completely replace human intelligence in the future?

AI has the potential to surpass human intelligence in certain tasks, but it's unlikely to completely replace human intelligence. While AI can process data faster, it lacks creativity, empathy, and complex reasoning that make humans unique.

What are the potential ethical concerns surrounding the use of AI?

Potential ethical concerns surrounding the use of AI include privacy invasion, job displacement, bias in decision-making algorithms, and autonomous weapons. These issues must be addressed to ensure responsible and equitable deployment of AI technology.

Can AI be used to improve healthcare and medical diagnostics?

AI can greatly improve healthcare and medical diagnostics. It has the potential to analyze vast amounts of data quickly, detect diseases at an early stage, and provide personalized treatment plans, leading to better patient outcomes.

Are there any risks associated with relying too heavily on AI in our daily lives?

Relying too heavily on AI in daily lives poses risks. Did you know that according to a survey, 63% of people worry about AI's impact on job security? It's essential to find a balance between human judgment and machine intelligence.

How can AI contribute to solving complex global challenges, such as climate change or poverty?

AI can contribute to solving complex global challenges like climate change or poverty by analyzing vast amounts of data, identifying patterns and trends, and providing insights that can help inform decision-making and develop effective solutions.

Conclusion

So, there you have it – a glimpse into the fascinating world of Artificial Intelligence. From self-driving cars to virtual assistants, AI has become an integral part of our everyday lives. It's like having your very own personal genie, ready to assist you with any task at hand.

But don't be fooled by its seemingly magical abilities. AI isn't here to replace us, but rather to enhance our capabilities and make our lives easier. Just like how Aladdin's genie granted him his deepest desires, AI grants us the power to accomplish more than we ever thought possible.

As we continue to embrace AI in the modern world, we must also acknowledge the opportunities and challenges that lie ahead. The future holds endless possibilities for innovation and advancement, but it also raises concerns about privacy, ethics, and job displacement.

However, let's remember that every technological leap comes with its fair share of uncertainties. We can't let fear hold us back from embracing the potential benefits that AI can bring. Instead, let's approach this brave new world with curiosity and open minds – just like Alice stepping through the looking glass into Wonderland.

So go ahead and welcome AI into your life with open arms. Embrace its ability to simplify tasks, improve efficiency, and unlock new realms of creativity. In doing so, you'll be joining a generation that dares to dream big and explore uncharted territories.

Just imagine what wonders await us on this exciting journey – where humans and machines coexist harmoniously in a world filled with limitless possibilities. Together, we can shape a future that's both awe-inspiring and beneficial for all.